BEADED ADORNMENTS

Creating New Looks for Clothes & Accessories

Elizabeth Gourley &
Ellen Talbott

Sterling Publishing Co., Inc.
New York

We would like to dedicate this book to the ancient person who first put a bead on a thread, and to our sugar hubbies, who made this all possible.

Acknowledgments
Our deepest thanks go to Sheila Barry, who believed in our ideas and helped make our dreams come true. We would also like to thank our families for doing without our attentions for so long, as well as Nonnie, for all she's done for us.

Photography by Michael Hnatov
Edited by Isabel Stein
Designed by Shelley Himmelstein

Library of Congress Cataloging-in-Publication Data
Gourley, Elizabeth.
    Beaded adornments : creating new looks for clothes & accessories / Elizabeth Gourley & Ellen Talbott.
        p. cm.
    Includes index.
    ISBN 1-4027-0998-6
    1. Beadwork. 2. Clothing and dress. 3. Dress accessories. 4. Fancy work. I. Talbott, Ellen. II. Title.
TT860.G682253 2005
745.58'2—dc22

                                                                    2004020421

10 9 8 7 6 5 4 3 2 1

Published by Sterling Publishing Co., Inc.
387 Park Avenue South, New York, NY 10016
©2005 by Elizabeth Gourley & Ellen Talbott
Distributed in Canada by Sterling Publishing
℅ Canadian Manda Group, 165 Dufferin Street
Toronto, Ontario, Canada M6K 3H6
Distributed in Great Britain by Chrysalis Books Group PLC
The Chrysalis Building, Bramley Road, London W10 6SP, England
Distributed in Australia by Capricorn Link (Australia) Pty. Ltd.
P.O. Box 704, Windsor, NSW 2756, Australia

Printed in China
All rights reserved

Sterling ISBN 1-4027-0998-6

For information about custom editions, special sales, premium and corporate purchases, please contact Sterling Special Sales Department at 800-805-5489 or specialsales@sterlingpub.com.

CONTENTS

1
Materials

· · · · ·

History of Beads

Just as music relies on the space between the notes, beadwork relies on the holes in the beads. We are two humble maestros of the bead who compose for you here in this book 31 melodious bead symphonies along with 24 embellishment techniques. We hope, through our book, to help you compose your own beaded works as your muse inspires you. Fashions may change, but the bead goes on … on shoes, shirts, skirts, hats, pants, purses….

Personal adornment in the form of beads has been around for more than 50,000 years and has influenced nearly every culture on Earth (Photo 1). Beads have served as symbols of wealth and power, as forms of communication, and have held magical and protective powers.

Stone-age people made beads from the objects around them, such as seeds, shells, bones, stones, teeth, and claws. Even before humans had tools, they had beads. In England, small fossil sponges with natural holes were found lying next to each other in graduated sizes in the form of a necklace. Once humans developed tools, they were able to make beads out of objects that didn't have natural holes. Animal-tooth beads and bone beads were found in France dating back to 38,000 BC, kangaroo bone beads dating from 13,000 BC were found in Australia, and in Africa they discovered ostrich eggshell beads that were about 12,000 years old.

As humans evolved, their bead-making techniques became more sophisticated, and bead artisans demanded rarer and more exotic materials. Trade routes expanded along with developing civilizations, and beads and materials for bead making became important trade items.

About 4600 years ago, the Indus Valley civilization, located where Pakistan and western India are today, was flourishing. In Harrapa, one of the largest cities of the Indus Valley, many beads, bead-making tools, and kilns have been unearthed. The earliest beads from this area were fashioned from soapstone, which is fairly soft and easy to drill. After the beads were drilled and polished, they were fired at high temperature, which changed the soapstone into a harder substance. Bead artisans also used stone and copper drills to make holes in stones such as agate and jasper. Because the drills and stones were of the same hardness, it was an arduous task to make holes in the small beads that the artisans of Harrapa used. Eventually, they developed a drill made of a very hard substance that scientists haven't been able to identify. These drills were unique to the Indus Valley and allowed the artisans to make beautiful carnelian beads that were prized as far away as Mesopotamia and Central Asia.

Photo 1. Kirdi beaded modesty apron from Northern Cameroon.

Photo 2. Northwest Indian moccasins.

Photo 3. Plains Indian beaded bag.

The first "manufactured" beads were made of faience, a type of ceramic composed of quartz sand, lime or loam, and a small amount of alkali. The faience was first melted in kilns and then reground and refired at high temperatures. Copper oxide or azurite was added to turn the faience blue, so it resembled lapis lazuli, which was highly prized and hard to obtain. Historians believe that faience was the forerunner of glass. The first true glass beads, from the Indus Valley, were made about 1700 BC, about 200 years earlier than the earliest ones found in Egypt. There is some evidence that true glass beads were made even earlier, about 2400 BC, in the region just south of the Caucasus Mountains in Russia.

A major turning point in the manufacture of small glass beads came around 200 BC in Arikamedu, India, where artisans developed a method of making drawn glass beads; this technique allowed the bead makers to produce hundreds of small beads at a time. The same technique is still used in India. These drawn glass beads were used by many countries to trade with East Africa for gold, ivory, and slaves.

Around 1200 AD, bead-making began to flourish in Venice. By the 1400s, India's glass bead-making industry was declining, and Venice took over the market. Glass seed beads as we know them today were being produced in Venice as early as the 1400s.

Because of their size, their ease of manufacture, and the demand, glass beads became a major item of trade with the New World, Indonesia, and Africa, yielding the Europeans huge profits. Although many beads were exported, Europeans themselves eventually used seed beads for embroidering on clothing and accessories. By the 1800s, seed beads had become popular for use in personal adornment in North and South America, Africa, Europe, Asia, Australia, Greenland, the Middle East, and Oceania (Photos 2 and 3).

Small glass beads are called by many names: seed beads, rocailles, pound beads (because they were once sold by the pound), and mani-doominens, the Anishnaabemowin (Ojibwe) word meaning "little seed that is a gift of the spirit." Seed beads have played an important role in the history of civilization.

Beads Today

Today glass beads come in an amazing number of colors, finishes, sizes, and shapes. Glass beads are broken down into categories: faceted glass beads, crystal beads, pressed glass beads, lampwork beads, Japanese tubular beads (Delica beads), charlotte beads, two-cuts, three-cuts, triangle beads, square beads, hex-cuts, bugle beads, and seed beads. Most of these glass beads lend themselves well to the embellishment of clothing and accessories.

Faceted glass beads have had one or more flat planes ground into their surface. Crystal beads are faceted, but are made of leaded glass (Photo 4). Pressed glass beads have been pressed in molds to make many different shapes, such as flowers, leaves, and fruit, of different sizes (Photo 5).

Lampwork beads are made individually, by hand, with a small torch and can be any shape or color the artist desires.

Photo 4. Crystal and glass faceted beads.

Photo 5. Pressed glass beads.

Japanese tubular beads (Delica beads) are precision-made and have a tubelike shape with large holes (Photo 6). The standard size is smaller than the standard size 11° seed bead and is comparable to a size 13° seed bead. They also come in a larger size that is close to a size 8° seed bead. *Note:* Throughout this book, the small size of Delica beads is used. Charlotte beads are actually a seed bead with one facet. They generally come in sizes 13° and 8°.

Two-cuts have two facets, and three-cuts have three or more random facets (Photo 7). There are approximately 17 size 6° seed beads per gram, approximately 115 size 11° seed beads per gram, and approximately 195 Delica beads per gram.

Hex-cuts are Japanese tubular beads made from a six-sided tube of glass. Triangle beads are small, triangle-shaped glass beads, and square beads are small square beads (Photo 8). There are also rectan-

Photo 6. Japanese tubular Delica beads.

Photo 7. Two-cuts (yellow and green) and hex beads (white and purple).

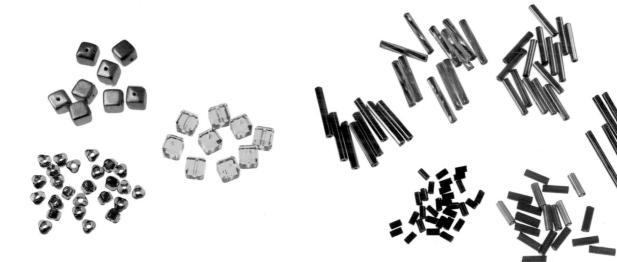

Photo 8. Triangle and square beads.

Photo 9. Bugle beads.

gular beads, which are sometimes called niblets. Bugle beads are long tubes of glass the same diameter as a seed bead but usually ⅛″ (3 mm) to 2″ (5 cm) long (Photo 9). White-heart beads are made of colored transparent glass with a lining of opaque white glass. These beads have a soft look and add depth of color to a design (Photo 10).

Seed beads are small round beads that come in sizes ranging from the largest, which are called crow beads and are 9 mm (⅜″), to the smallest, size 22°, which are as small as a grain of sand. Sizes 18° through 22° haven't been made since the late 1800s, but they can still be found. The standard size for seed beads is 11°.

Glass beads are made from different types of glass. Transparent glass lets the light through and gives the color of the bead depth. It has a tendency to make the beads recede into a design. Opaque glass doesn't let light through and makes the color of the bead stand out. Greasy glass is in between transparent and opaque; some light gets through. Opal glass lets more light through than greasy glass, but is not transparent. Satin glass has a velvety

appearance caused by tiny bubbles in the glass. Transparent or opal glass beads are sometimes lined in silver, which gives the beads a sparkling, reflective quality. Silver-lined beads have either a square hole or a round hole. The square hole is used to add more sparkle. Glass beads can also be color-lined. These beads are usually made with clear transparent glass, and all the color

Photo 10. White-heart beads.

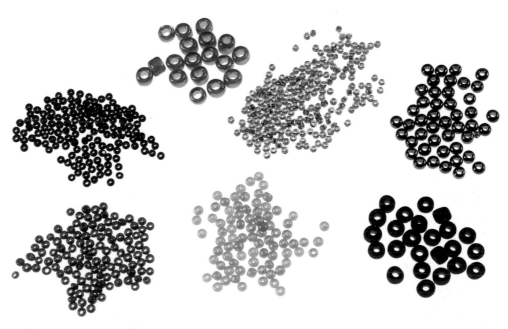

Photo 11. Seed beads (counterclockwise from upper right): Light green, size 15°; green, size 5°; red, size 14°; purple, size 11°; pink, size 10°; blue, size 6°; metallic, size 8°.

comes from the lining of the hole; some color-lined beads are made with a transparent color bead and a different color lining. These beads look smaller than they are, and the color can be quite brilliant.

Beads can be finished in several ways. Iridescent finish is also called AB (for aurora borealis), iris, or rainbow. It is achieved by putting metal salts on the hot glass, which causes a rainbow sheen to appear. Matte finish is dull and frosted; it softens the color of the bead. Luster finish is shiny. A pearl finish creates a milky shine. Metallic finishes make the beads look like metal, an effect achieved by applying a galvanized or painted coating. Dyed beads are made with a surface colorant. So many combinations, colors, and finishes exist (and are being developed) that the choices are infinite.

Other Supplies

Bead embellishment requires few supplies. Besides the beads (and the clothing and accessories to put them on), basically all you need are needles, thread, hoops, looms, and embroidery scissors. Most of these supplies can be found at bead, craft, fabric, or needlework stores.

Thread

For bead-embroidery, off-loom bead weaving, or bead loomwork, nylon monofilament thread such as Nymo™ is a popular choice. It lends itself well to beadwork, it is strong and rot resistant, and it comes in many sizes and colors. Size 000 is very fine, and size FFF is very heavy.

The most common sizes are 0, B, D, and F. Size D is a versatile size and works well with size 11° seed beads.

For tambour work, ari work, and tatting, cotton crochet thread and cotton tatting thread work well. Cotton crochet thread is basically the same thing as tatting thread, only thicker. Tatting thread comes in sizes 70 and 80, which are very fine. Crochet thread usually comes in sizes 60 through 10, with 10 being the thickest and 60 being the thinnest (Photo 12). The thread choice is made depending on the look you want to achieve, the weight of the fabric, and the size of the beads and needles you are using (Photo 13).

Needles

There are a variety of needles for beading, including beading needles, loomwork beading needles, twisted beading needles, embroidery needles, tatting needles, and tambour needles.

Beading needles are slender and straight with very small eyes, so the beads will slip over them easily. They come in several lengths and thicknesses. The most common lengths are 1¼″ (3 cm), 2″ (5 cm), and 3″ (8 cm). They come in sizes 10 (thick) to 16 (very fine). The most popular sizes are 11 and 12, which work well with size 11° seed beads (Photo 14). Bead loomwork needles have blunt tips so they

Photo 12. Crochet cotton and tatting thread.

Photo 13. Beading threads.

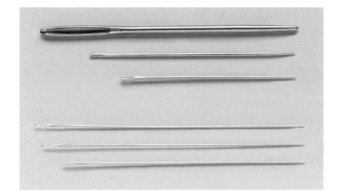

Photo 14. Beading needles and embroidery needles.

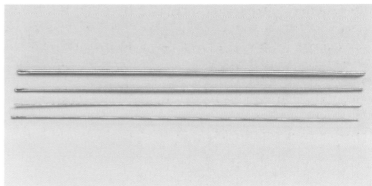

Photo 15. Tatting needles. Size 8, extra fine; size 7, fine; size 5, medium; size 3, heavy.

don't split the warp threads and are 5″ (13 cm) and 7½″ (19 cm) long. They usually come in size 10 because of their length.

The twisted-wire beading needle is made of a length of wire twisted back on itself; a large loop at the top makes the eye. It is a great needle for thicker thread that won't go through the eye of a regular beading needle. The eye of a twisted-wire needle collapses when it is passed through the bead hole, so it fits through quite easily. Twisted-wire beading needles come in sizes very fine, fine, medium, and heavy.

Embroidery needles come in handy in bead embellishment for sewing the beadwork to the garment. Tatting needles are 5″ (13 cm) long and slender, with a blunt tip (Photo 15). They come in sizes 8 (extra fine), 7 (fine), 5 (medium), and 3 (heavy). They also come in thicker sizes for yarn tatting.

Tambour Hooks

Tambour hooks are made up of the tambour handle and the tambour needle. The tambour handle is usually made of wood, with a thumb-screw at the top used to tighten the needle into the handle. Tambour needles come in short and long lengths, depending on the type of handle used. They come in a variety of diameters, from fine, size 70, 0.03″ (.75 mm) diameter, to thick, size 130, .052″ (1.3 mm) diameter. Size 70 needles work well with size 11° seed beads, for the ari stitch. Tambour needles have a sharp barb at the tip for puncturing the fabric and catching the thread. Tambour hooks are also called ari hooks (Photo 16). Photo 17 shows a tambour-beaded moth design on a skirt.

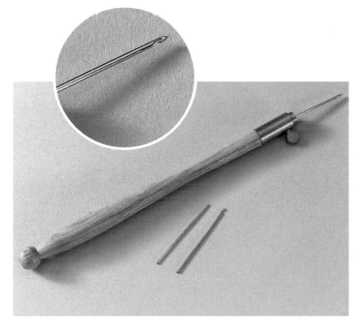

Photo 16. Tambour handle and needles.

Photo 17. Tambour-beaded moth design on a skirt.

Tambour Hoops and Frames

Embroidery hoops and tambour hoops are basically the same. They come in sizes from 3″ (8 cm) diameter to large quilter's hoops. Sizes 7″ (18 cm) to 10″ (25 cm) are the most commonly used ones for bead embellishment. Their purpose is to hold the fabric taut while one is embroidering or tambouring (Photo 18). Tambour frames hold a 10″ (25 cm) embroidery hoop and allow for a 360° rotation of the hoop. It is essential to view the back of your work when doing bead tambour work, so this rotation feature is very handy.

Bead Looms

Looms are used to hold the warp (up-and-down) threads of weaving projects. There are several kinds of loom available (Photo 19). You can also make your own loom. The loom you choose depends on the length and width of your project. Photo 20 shows a belt whose design was made on a bead loom.

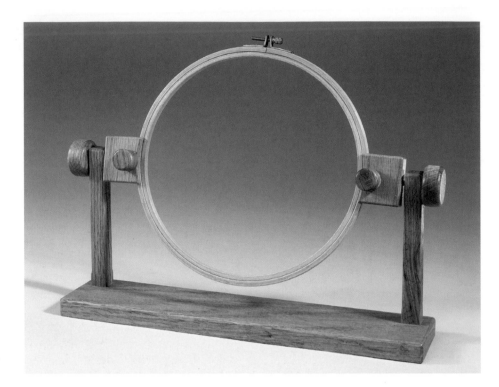

Photo 18. Tambour frame and stand.

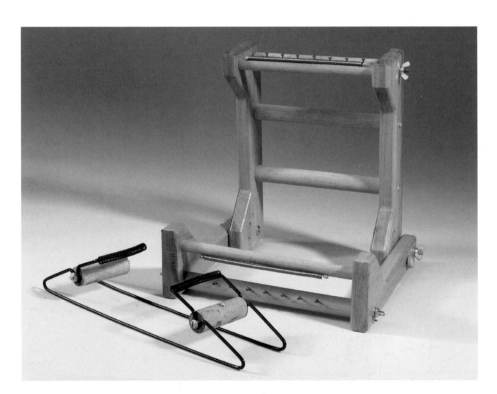

Photo 19. Bead looms.

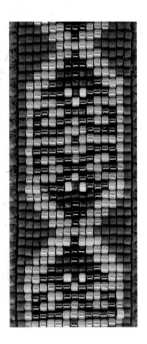

Photo 20. The purple flower design on this belt was made on a bead loom.

Transfer Tools and Methods

There are several ways to transfer a design onto the garment to be beaded. The one you choose depends on the article to be beaded, the type and weight of the fabric, and personal preference. Never use pencil when marking fabric or tracing the design onto tracing paper because the graphite will discolor the fabric, especially light-colored fabric. Graphite is nearly impossible to remove. You can use water-soluble fabric markers instead.

Pounce Powder Method

The pounce powder method requires a pounce pad (which is a small wooden or plastic handle with felt pads on the end), pounce powder, tracing paper, a needle or pin large enough to make holes that the powder will go through, and a fabric marker, the water-soluble kind. Begin by tracing the design onto tracing paper. Then place the paper on a soft surface and with the needle or pin poke holes in the paper all along the design lines. Place the tracing paper over the fabric to be beaded. Tape the paper in place with masking tape. Then dip the pounce pad into the pounce powder, and rub the pad over the design lines until the powder fills all the holes. Remove the paper and mark over the dotted lines with the fabric marker. This method is accurate and works well with most fabric types and weights; however, it is time-consuming and doesn't work well with an intricate design. If there are too many design lines that are too close together, the tracing paper falls apart. The beaded design shown in Photo 21 was transferred by the pounce powder method.

Trace-and-Baste Method

This is a simple method that works well with all fabric types and even with intricate designs. Trace the design onto the tracing paper, and then baste the paper over the fabric at the spot to be beaded. Bead right over the tracing paper, following the design lines. If you want, you can remove the tracing paper after all the outlines are beaded and then fill in the rest of the beads without the paper. The paper comes away fairly easily when you rip it away from the beads. In small, hard-to-reach areas, sharp tweezers are a handy tool. The beads and their placement will not be damaged by ripping the paper out from under them.

Heat-Transfer Pencil Method

A heat-transfer pencil is an easy way to transfer designs to fabric; however, it can't be removed and doesn't work well on some fabrics. Trace the design onto a piece of paper with the heat-transfer pencil.

Photo 21. Lotus design (left) was transferred by the pounce powder method to create the beaded flower at right.

Photo 22. Design-transfer tools. Left: Dressmakers' carbon paper and tracing wheels. Top center, pounce powder and pouncing tool.

(When the design is transferred to the fabric, it will be flopped, so if you don't want a mirror image, you must trace the design twice so it will be facing the right way when transferred.) Then place the paper face down onto the fabric to be beaded. Iron the paper until the design transfers onto the fabric.

Template Method

If the design is simple, you can trace it onto tracing paper, transfer it to card stock paper, and then cut out around the outline, making a template of the design. Tape the template in place, using folded-over pieces of masking tape. With a fabric marker, trace around the template. This method works best if you place the fabric to be beaded on a hard surface.

Dressmaker's Carbon Paper Method

This method uses dressmaker's carbon paper and a tracing wheel or a ballpoint pen. Place the fabric to be beaded right side up on a hard surface. Then place the carbon paper face down on the fabric. Put a tracing of the design on top of the carbon paper, and then, with a tracing wheel or a ballpoint pen, trace around the design lines, pressing really hard (these only work well with a very simple design). The carbon paper method works well on lightweight woven fabric such as quilter's cotton. For knitted fabrics such as cotton T-shirt material, it doesn't work as well. Pick a color of fabric carbon paper that contrasts well with your fabric. You might have to go over the lines with a fabric marker if they are too light.

Transfer-Fabric Method

Use a sheer transfer material or net instead of tracing paper, and trace the design onto the transfer fabric, using a fabric marker. Then pin the transfer fabric to the fabric to be beaded and trace over the design on the transfer fabric with the fabric marker. The material or net is sheer enough that the fabric marker will mark through it and onto the fabric of the garment to be beaded. This is a quick and easy method that works well on all fabric types. It works best if you place the fabric to be beaded on a hard surface.

2
Techniques

Basic Stitches of Bead Embroidery

Sewing beads onto clothing is an ancient craft. Ivory beads fashioned from wooly mammoth tusks were used to adorn clothing more than 25,000 years ago. The famous archeological site of Sungir, about 90 miles (150 km) east of Moscow, near the city of Vladimir, has yielded the oldest known example of beads arranged on human remains as if they had been sewn to clothing. Sungir was the northernmost settlement in Europe of *Homo sapiens sapiens* or Cro-Magnons from the Upper Paleolithic period. The three best-preserved remains were found literally covered in rows of ivory beads. They were also wearing fox-tooth beads, pendants painted red, and polished ivory bracelets. It's interesting to think that early humans from the Ice Ages had the same fascination with beads, personal adornment, and art that we have today.

The following techniques will help you rival the Cro-Magnon's bead-embroidery skills. Any embroidery stitch can be modified to accommodate beads. This book discusses eight of the basic embroidery stitches. When bead-embroidering on finished garments, it is not always necessary to use an embroidery hoop. If the fabric is sturdy enough, and if you are careful to avoid puckering, you don't need to use an embroidery hoop. No matter what, you do need to use a hoop when couching.

Photo 1. Bead-embroidered Victorian cuffs.

Seed Stitch

The seed stitch is the most basic of all the bead-embroidery stitches (Fig. 1).

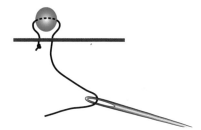

1. The seed stitch.

1. Thread the beading needle with a length of beading thread. Tie a knot at the end and pass the needle up through the fabric to be beaded.

2. String on 1 bead, and then pass the needle down through the fabric one bead length away from where the thread came out of the fabric.

3. Repeat this stitch randomly over the fabric, with the beads far apart or close together or in evenly spaced lines, depending on the look you are trying to achieve.

Stacked Seed Stitch

The stacked seed stitch (Fig. 2) is similar to the basic fringe stitch, except the stacked seed stitch is made in the middle of the fabric instead of at the edge of the fabric. The stacked seed stitch adds dimension to the otherwise two-dimensional fabric.

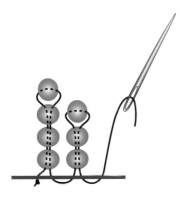

2. The stacked seed stitch.

1. Thread the beading needle with a length of beading thread. Tie a knot at the end and pass the needle up through the fabric to be beaded.

2. String on anywhere from 2 to 7 beads. If you use more than about 7 beads, the stitch will not stand upright and will tend to flop over; however, if that is the look you want, go for it!

3. Skip the last bead strung on and pass the needle back through the other beads. Pass the needle down through the fabric right next to where the thread came out of the fabric and pull the thread tight.

4. Repeat this stitch using varying bead numbers, and space them according to your design.

Backstitch

The backstitch is useful for outlining areas and for making straight and curved lines, such as vines or stems. It can also be used to fill in areas.

1. Thread the beading needle with a length of beading thread. Tie a knot at the end, and pass the needle up through the fabric to be beaded.

2. String on from 1 to 3 beads (the straighter the line, the more beads you use; for curvier lines, use one bead at a time).

3. Pass the needle down through the fabric at the end of the beads. Then pass the needle up through the fabric in between the last two beads strung on, and pass the needle back through the last bead strung on.

4. Repeat as often as desired. Figure 3 shows groups of two beads being stitched on.

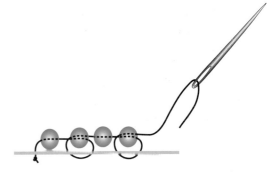

3. The backstitch.

Photo 2. French bead-embroidered bag.

Photo 3. Sheep design uses looped backstitch.

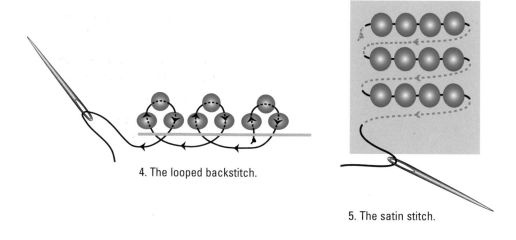

4. The looped backstitch.

5. The satin stitch.

Looped Backstitch

In the looped backstitch, the size of the stitch is smaller than the length of the beads, causing the beads to form a loop (Fig. 4 and Photo 3).

1. Thread the beading needle with a length of beading thread. Tie a knot at the end, and pass the needle up through the fabric a stitch length away from the end of the line to be beaded. Always start at the right end of the line, if you are right-handed.

2. String on 3 beads or any odd number of beads, and then pass the needle down through the fabric at the start of the design line. The smaller the stitch, the more the beads will loop.

3. Pass the needle up through the fabric a stitch length away from where the thread first came out of the fabric. String on 3 beads, and then pass the needle down through the fabric right next to the first stitch.

4. Repeat as often as necessary. Make sure to leave a small space between each stitch so the fabric will lie flat; if the stitches are too close together, the fabric will bunch up.

Satin Stitch

The satin stitch is good for filling in large areas (Photo 4).

1. Thread the beading needle with a length of beading thread. Tie a knot at the end, and pass the needle up through the fabric to be beaded.

2. String on the desired amount of beads. For this example we used 4 beads. Push the beads down the thread until they touch the fabric, and then pass the needle down through the fabric at the end of the line of beads. (If you pass the needle down through the fabric at a distance longer than the line of beads, the beads will be loose along the thread and the thread will show. If you pass the needle down through the fabric at a distance shorter than the line of beads, the beads will loop up.) This forms the first stitch.

3. Pass the needle up through the fabric to the side of the beads at a point that is a bead width from the beginning of the first stitch. String on 4 beads, and then pass the needle down through the fabric at a point that is a bead width from the end of the first stitch. The stitches are parallel to each other (Fig. 5).

4. Repeat the desired number of times.

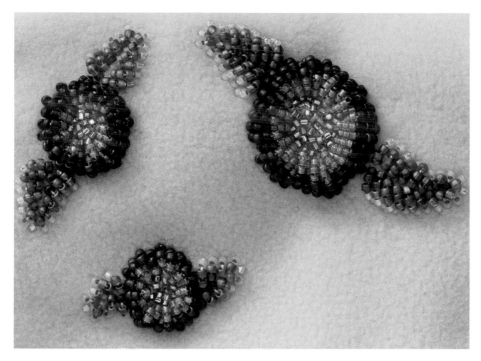

Photo 4. Petals and leaves are done in the satin stitch.

Photo 5. Native American pouch with lane stitching.

Lane Stitch

The lane stitch (Fig. 6) is a variation of the satin stitch. It is good for filling in large areas with beads. The Native Americans use this stitch for quite a bit of their bead-embroidery work (Photo 5).

1. Thread the beading needle with a length of beading thread. Tie a knot at the end, and pass the needle up through the fabric to be beaded.

2. String on the desired amount of beads. For this example we used 4 beads. Push the beads down the thread until they touch the fabric, and then make a small stitch, perpendicular to the line of beads, next to the last bead strung on. This makes the first stitch.

3. String on 4 beads, push them down until they touch the fabric, and then make a small stitch next to the beginning of the first stitch.

4. String on 4 beads, and then make a small stitch next to the beginning of the second stitch.

5. Repeat in this manner until the desired length is reached.

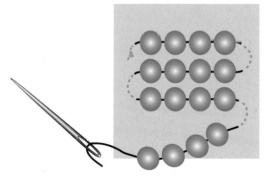

6. The lane stitch.

Detached Chain Stitch

The detached chain stitch is handy when you are making leaves or petals of flowers (Fig. 7).

1. Thread the beading needle with a length of beading thread. Tie a knot at the end, and pass the needle up through the fabric to be beaded.

2. String on 7 beads or any odd number of beads, and then pass the needle down through the fabric at a point right next to where the thread came out of the fabric. Pull tight. This forms a loop.

3. Pass the needle up through the fabric right under the fourth (or middle) bead of the loop. Pass the needle through this bead, and then pass the needle down through the fabric. This holds the loop onto the fabric.

4. Repeat this stitch in a circle to form a flower, or in rows, or randomly spaced, depending on the look desired.

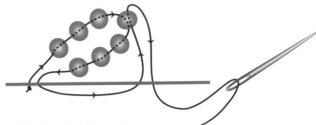

7. The detached chain stitch.

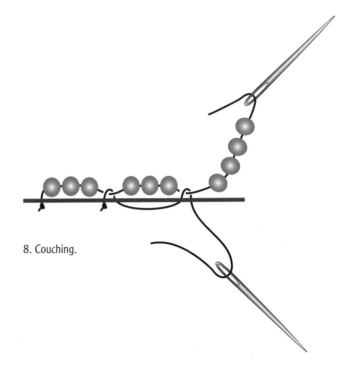

8. Couching.

Couching

In couching, rather than sewing the beads to the fabric, you are in effect tacking the thread of a string of beads onto the fabric (Fig. 8). Couching can be done with one or two needles. An embroidery hoop is a necessity in couching. The method used in this book is two-needle couching; an example is shown in Photo 6.

1. Thread each of the two needles with a length of beading thread. Make a knot on the end of both threads. Use a long beading needle for the beaded thread and a short beading needle for the thread used to tack down the beaded thread. This makes it easy to distinguish between the two threads.

Photo 6. Detail of couched leather belt.

2. Pass the long needle up through the fabric at the beginning of the design line. String the desired amount of beads onto the thread with the long needle. Push the beads down to the fabric.

3. Pass the short needle up through the fabric at a point about 3 beads from the beginning of the bead line.

Pass the short needle down through the fabric on the other side of the bead thread. This tacks down the strand of beads.

4. Repeat, using the short needle, about every 3 beads or so. Add more beads to the long beading needle thread as needed.

Beaded Chain Stitch: Tambour and Ari

The art of chain stitch embroidery, worked on a frame with a hook, has been around for a long time. No one knows for sure, but some say that it began in ancient China or the Indus River Valley in India. It was and is a very popular form of embroidery in India, Pakistan, Turkey, and other countries of the Middle East. By the 1700s, if not earlier, chain stitch embroidery had been introduced to Europe and became known as tambour (French for *drum*) embroidery because of the drumlike shape of the embroidery frame used. Beads were incorporated into the stitches in the late 1800s.

In the west (Europe and the United States), the hook used in chain stitch embroidery is called a tambour needle; in the Middle East and India, the hook is known as an *ari*. In tambour beading, the beads must be prestrung on the thread. The project is worked with the wrong side up, and the chain stitch is formed on the wrong side of the fabric; the beads are caught in the single-thread stitch formed on the right side. In ari beading, the beads are not prestrung; they are placed one by one on the hook. The project is worked with the right side up; you slide the beads down the hook onto the chain, and they are thus held onto the fabric. The wrong side has the single-thread stitch with no beads on it. For both tambour and ari beading, it is a good idea to practice the chain stitch without beads until you get the rhythm down. It is frustrating at first, but soon becomes fun and easy. Both techniques require a tambour hoop.

Tambour Beading

1. Transfer the design onto the wrong side of the work. Place the work wrong side up in the tambour hoop and stretch tight. Make sure the design is in the middle of the hoop and is facing up. Then put the hoop in the stand. Tighten the tambour needle into the tambour handle with the hook facing the screw on the handle, so it is easy to see where the hook is.

2. Using a twisted beading needle, string the desired amount of beads onto the thread ball. (It's better to string on a few more beads than you think you will need because it is

Photo 7. Tambour embroidery on lace.

easier to take off extra beads when you are through than to run out of beads and have to add more to the ball of thread.) Keep the ball of beaded thread under the hoop.

3. Holding the tambour hook with your dominant hand, puncture the fabric with the tambour needle (making sure the hook is pointing away from you) at the beginning of one of the lines of the design.

a. Turn the hook 90° counterclockwise, and with the other hand under the hoop, secure a loop of thread onto the hook (Fig. 1).

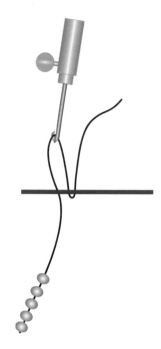

2. Thread end pulled through the fabric, viewed from opposite the beader.

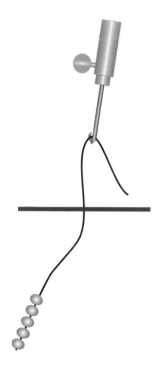

3. Loop of thread pulled through the fabric, viewed from opposite the beader.

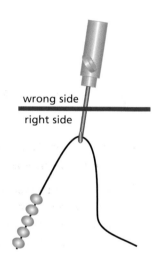

1. Securing a loop of thread onto the hook under the fabric.

b. Twist the hook counterclockwise another 90° so it is facing you, pull the needle out of the fabric, and then pull the thread end through the fabric until there is about an 8" (20 cm) length of thread (Fig. 2). The hardest part of tambour stitch is getting the hook to come out without catching on the fabric. If the piece is kept stretched very tight in the hoop, and if the pressure on the fabric as you pull the thread through is kept away from the hook, it doesn't seem to catch as much.

c. Puncture the fabric in a spot near the thread end (make sure the hook is pointing away from you.) Turn the hook 90° counterclockwise and with the hand under the hoop, secure a loop of thread onto the hook. Then twist the hook counterclockwise another 90° so it is facing you, and pull the hook and the loop through the fabric (Fig. 3).

d. Remove the hook from the loop, put the thread end through the loop, and pull tight (Fig. 4). This anchors the thread to the fabric.

4. Now that the thread is anchored, you can start the first stitch. Slide a bead up the thread until it touches the fabric.

a. Puncture the fabric with the needle at a point a little more distant than a bead width from the anchor stitch. (Make sure the hook is pointing away from you.)

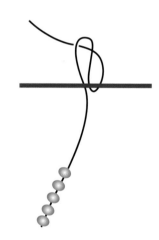

4. Anchoring the thread to the fabric.

b. Twist the hook 90° counterclockwise, and secure a loop of thread onto the hook. Make sure that the bead is between the fabric and the loop.

c. Twist the hook another 90° counterclockwise, so it is facing you, and pull the loop through the fabric (Fig. 5). Pull the stitch tight by jerking the needle back and forth.

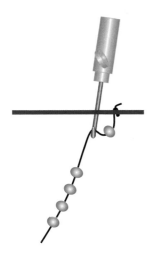

5. First beaded stitch.

d. With the needle in the loop, puncture the fabric again, leaving a space a little longer than a bead width.

e. Slide a bead up to the fabric, secure a loop of thread onto the hook, and pull through the fabric and the loop. Tighten the stitch (Fig. 6).

f. Keep stitching with the beads until you come to the end of the design line. Make sure to tighten each stitch, and check the under side of the hoop every so often to make

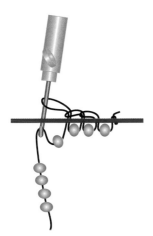

6. Beaded tambour stitch.

sure there are no loose stitches or twisted beads.

g. At the end of the design line, anchor the thread by making a small stitch without a bead and then pulling the loop until it is about 8″ (20 cm) long. Then cut the thread loop at the top and pull tight.

h. With the hand under the hoop, pull the thread ball so the cut thread comes out of the fabric. Remove any excess beads from the thread ball.

i. Tambour-stitch along the rest of the design lines, stringing beads and changing thread for each line and color.

5. When you are all done, tie off every thread end with a small knot for extra security, and weave all the thread ends into the chains using a size 10 crochet hook. Cut off the excess thread. Take the project out of the frame and enjoy!

Ari Beading

1. Transfer the design onto the right side of the work. Then place the work right side up into the hoop, and stretch it tight. Make sure the design is in the middle of the hoop, and place the hoop into the tambour stand.

2. Tighten the tambour needle into the tambour handle with the hook facing the screw on the handle, so it is easy to see where the hook is.

a. Place the ball of thread under the hoop. Hold the thread in your nondominant hand, and hold the ari hook in your dominant hand. Anchor the thread the same way as is done in tambour beading. (In ari all the thread ends will be on the right side of the work and must be moved to the wrong side of the work later.)

3. With the hook facing away from you, puncture the fabric at a point adjacent to the anchor thread.

a. Twist the hook 90° counterclockwise, and secure a loop of thread onto the hook (Fig. 7). Twist the hook 90° counterclockwise again, so it is facing you. Pull the needle and the loop out of the fabric.

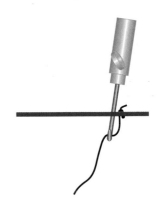

7. Securing a loop of thread onto the hook under the fabric.

b. Take the needle out of the loop, and put a bead onto the needle.

c. Put the hook back on the loop, and slide the bead down the needle and onto the loop of thread (Fig. 8). Push the bead down so it touches the fabric.

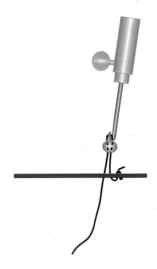

8. Sliding the bead onto the thread loop.

d. Keep the needle in the loop, and puncture the fabric at a point a little bit more distant than the bead.

e. Secure a loop of thread onto the hook, and pull the loop up through the fabric and through the loop with the bead on it (Fig. 9). Pull the stitch tight by jerking the needle back and forth.

4. Continue in this fashion to make ari chain stitches along the rest of the design lines, changing thread for each line. A new thread must be started every time lines start or stop.

5. There will be many thread ends, and they will get in the way, so every so often they must be moved to the wrong side of the work. (Use an embroidery needle.) Make a knot for extra security, weave the thread ends into the stitches, and cut off the excess.

Photo 8 is an example of ari beading.

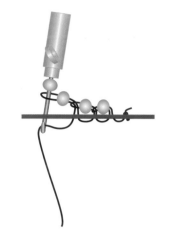

9. Beaded ari chain stitch.

Photo 8. Ari-beaded egret design.

Beaded Fringes

Photo 9. Several kinds of fringe on hair elastics.

Flapper dresses of the roaring '20s were famous for their beaded fringes. Flappers, young women who were rebelling against the stodgy Victorian morals of their parents, wore dresses that had knee-length straight skirts and a boyish look. The dresses were often covered in fringe, so that when the flappers danced, and dance they did, their movements would be intensified by the swinging fringe. Beads made a great fringe; their weight and sparkle enhance any movement. Clothes today can be beautifully enhanced by beaded fringes and edgings.

There are many fringe and edging techniques. We hope you will be inspired by the instructions for some of them in this book to discover your own fringe or edge style.

Basic Fringe

The basic fringe technique is simple and versatile.

1. Thread a beading needle with a length of beading thread, knot the end, and pass the needle through the edge of the fabric to be fringed. String on as many beads as desired.

2. Skip the last bead strung on, pass the needle back through all the other beads, and pass the needle through the fabric edge (Fig. 1). For extra security, you may wish to make a knot after each fringe.

3. To pull the fringe up tight against the fabric, you must first make sure that the end bead is tight up against the beads. If you just pull on the thread at the end of the fringe to tighten it, the fringe will only tighten up to the end bead;

don't make it too tight, or it won't dangle freely.

4. For a little excitement, try using a charm or accent bead for the end bead. Change colors to make a pattern, or try varying the length of each fringe. Repeat as many times as desired.

1. Basic fringe.

Branched Fringe

This technique (Fig. 2) is a variation of the basic fringe.

1. Thread a beading needle with a length of beading thread, knot the end, and pass the needle through the edge of the fabric to be fringed. String on 4 beads. The bead number can vary depending on the design. The numbers used here are examples.

2. Skip the fourth bead strung on, and pass the needle back through the third and second bead.

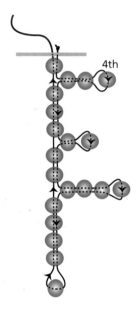

2. Branched fringe.

3. String on 5 beads, skip the last bead strung on, and pass the needle back through the second to last bead strung on. (Make sure you keep the beads tight up against each other as you go, or it will be difficult to tighten the fringe.)

4. String on 6 beads, skip the last bead strung on, and pass the needle back through the next 3 beads.

5. String on 5 beads, skip the last bead strung on, and pass the needle back through the 10 beads that form the base strand.

6. When you are finished, the branches will flop to both sides of

the fringe and won't be all on one side. Tighten the same way as for the basic fringe. You can make your fringe sparse or full by adding or subtracting branches. Repeat as many times as desired.

Looped Branch Fringe

This technique is a fancy version of the branched fringe. For this example we used green seed beads and blue bugle beads (Fig. 3).

1. Knot the end of the thread, and pass the needle through the edge of the fabric to be fringed.

2. *String on 6 green beads, 1 bugle bead, 3 green beads, and 1 bugle bead. Pass the needle back through the 6th, 5th, and 4th green beads strung on.* This forms the first loop. Repeat between the asterisks 2 times.

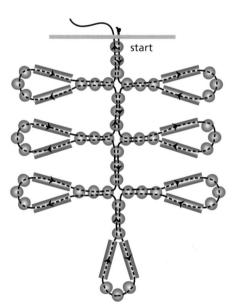

3. Looped branch fringe.

3. String on 3 green beads, 1 bugle bead, 3 green beads, and 1 bugle bead. Pass the needle back through the first 3 green beads just strung on.

4. **String on 3 green beads, 1 bugle bead, 3 green beads, and 1 bugle bead. Pass the needle back

through the first 3 green beads strung on and up through the next 3 green beads of the base strand.** Repeat between the double asterisks 2 times.

5. Tie off and begin the next fringe. Repeat as desired. You can vary this fringe by substituting other beads for the bugle beads or by changing the amount of beads used on the base strand or on the branches. Use your imagination.

Double Fringe

This fringe is a variation of a vertical net stitch. We used green and blue seed beads here for clarity (Fig. 4).

1. Knot the end of the thread, and pass the needle through the edge of the fabric to be fringed.

2. String on 1 green, 3 blue, 1 green, 3 blue, 1 green, 3 blue, 1 green, and 1 blue bead. Pass the needle back through the last green bead strung on.

4. Double fringe.

Photo 9. Twisted fringe on a knitted scarf.

3. String on 3 blue beads, and pass the needle back through the third green bead strung on.

4. String on 3 blue beads, and pass the needle back through the second green bead strung on.

5. String on 3 blue beads. Pass the needle back through the first green bead strung on. Pass the needle through the fabric and tie off.

6. Repeat as many times as desired. You can vary this fringe by using more base strand beads between the "holes," by making more or fewer holes, or by making smaller or larger holes.

Twisted Fringe

Twisted fringe is made with two beading needles (Fig. 5).

1. Thread a needle onto each end of a length of thread. Pass both needles through the edge of the fabric to be fringed. Then pass both

needles through the loop made by the thread, and pull tight, making a lark's head knot.

2. Pass both needles through 1 green bead. Then string 18 blue seed beads onto each needle separately. Make sure the beads are tight up against the fabric, and then twist the two strands around each other 4 or 5 times.

3. Pass both needles through 1 green bead and 1 blue bead.

4. Pass both needles through the last green bead strung on. Then string 18 blue seed beads onto each needle separately.

5. Twist the two strands around each other 4 or 5 times, and pass both the needles through the first green bead strung on.

6. Make a stitch in the fabric with both needles, and then repeat as many times as desired. Be creative in the numbers, shapes, colors, and sizes of beads.

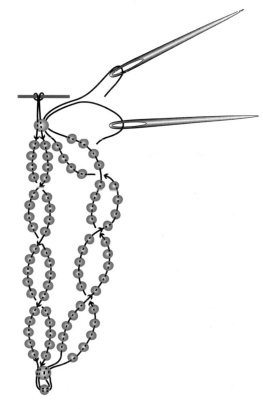

5. Twisted fringe.

Beaded Edgings

Zipper-Stitch Edging

This is a popular, compact, basic edging used in beadwork by Native Americans (Fig. 1).

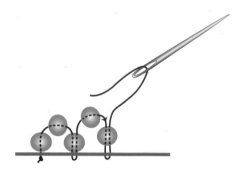

1. Zipper-stitch edging.

1. Tie a knot on the end of the thread, and pass the needle through the fabric to be edged.

2. String on 3 green beads. Make a small stitch on the edge of the fabric about ⅛″ (3 mm) from the place where the thread is coming out of the fabric, and pass the needle back through the third bead strung on.

3. *String on 2 beads. Make a small stitch in the fabric about ⅛″ (3 mm) from the place where the thread is coming out of the fabric, and pass the needle back through the last bead strung on.*

4. Repeat between the asterisks as many times as desired.

Daisy Edging

This is a variation of the zipper-stitch. For clarity, we used blue, green, and yellow seed beads. Many kinds or colors of beads can be used for a variety of different looks (Fig. 2).

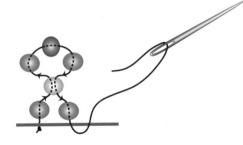

2. Daisy edging.

1. Tie a knot on the end of the thread, and pass the needle through the fabric to be edged.

2. *String on 1 blue, 1 yellow, 1 blue, 1 green, and 1 blue bead, and then pass the needle back through the yellow bead. String on 1 blue bead, and then make a small stitch in the fabric.*

3. Repeat between the asterisks as many times as desired.

V Edging

This edging covers a lot of ground in no time. For clarity, we used blue and green seed beads. The color, size, shape, and number of beads you choose to use are limitless (Fig. 3).

1. Tie a knot on the end of the thread, and pass the needle through the fabric to be edged.

2. *String on 4 blue, 1 green, and 1 blue bead. Pass the needle back through the green bead, and then string on 4 blue beads. Leave about a ¼″ (6 mm) space, and then make a small stitch.*

3. Repeat between the asterisks as many times as you like. The space might have to be adjusted according to the number of beads used and the steepness of the V desired.

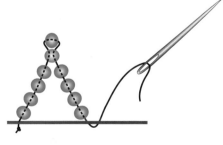

3. V edging.

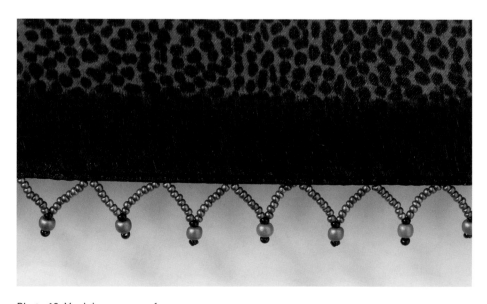

Photo 10. V edging on a scarf.

Bead Netting: Vertical and Horizontal

Bead netting is an ancient beading technique. In 1923, a bead-netted dress about 4400 years old was found in a tomb in Qau, Egypt. Many of the 3000 faience beads used in the dress were similar in shape to modern bugle beads. It was also a common practice in ancient Egypt to cover a mummy with a net of blue faience beads over the final layer of linen. For many centuries, native South Americans have made beautiful bead-netted collars. Netting was and is a popular beading technique in many African countries as well (Photo 11).

Vertical Netting

Vertical netting is an easy stitch to master. The rows are vertical, hence the name, and they have two sides: the downward side of the row and the upward side of the row. Vertical netting works well with all kinds of beads, including seed, bugle, and accent. The number of beads in each row can be changed, so the holes in the net can be large, small, or anywhere in between. For clarity, we used blue and green seed beads here.

■ Make the base strand (Fig. 1, top horizontal row) by stringing on the desired number of beads. Skip the last bead strung on, and pass the needle back through the next two beads on the base strand.

Row 1, downward side (Fig. 1):
a. String on 1 green, 2 blue, 1 green, 2 blue, 1 green, 2 blue, 1 green, 2 blue, 1 green, and 1 blue bead. Now you are finished with the downward side of row 1.

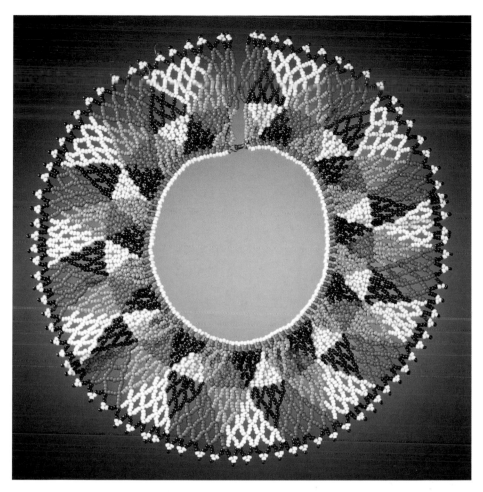

Photo 11. South American netted collar.

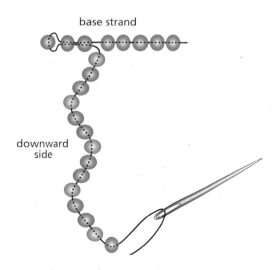

1. Downward side of the first row.

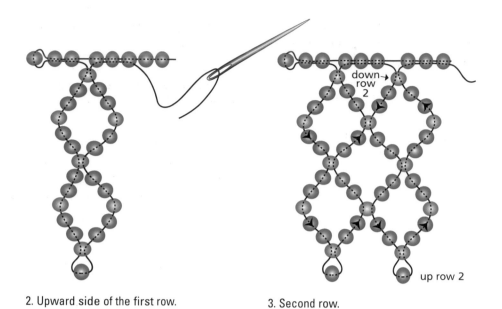

2. Upward side of the first row.

3. Second row.

up row 2

down row 2

4. Making the row longer.

Row 1, upward side (Fig. 2):

a. Pass the needle back through the last green bead from the downward side of the row.

b. String on 2 blue, 1 green, and 2 blue beads (Fig. 3). Pass the needle back through the third green bead strung on the downward side of the row.

c. String on 2 blue, 1 green, and 2 blue beads. Pass the needle back through the first green bead strung on the downward side of the row. Pass the needle back through the next 3 beads on the base strand.

Row 2, downward side (Fig. 3):

a. String on 1 green and 2 blue beads, and pass the needle back through the last green bead strung onto the upward side of the previous row.

b. String on 2 blue, 1 green, and 2 blue beads (Fig. 3). Pass the needle back through the first green bead

strung onto the upward side of the previous row.

c. String on 2 blue, 1 green, and 1 blue bead. Now you are finished with the downward side of row 2.

Row 2, upward side (Fig. 3):

a. Pass the needle back through the last green bead from the downward side of the row.

b. String on 2 blue, 1 green, and 2 blue beads. Pass the needle back through the third green bead strung on the downward side of the row.

c. String on 2 blue, 1 green, and 2 blue beads. Pass the needle back through the first green bead strung on the downward side of the row. Pass the needle back through the next 3 beads on the base strand (Fig. 3).

Remaining Rows:

■ Repeat row 2 instructions (downward and upward sides) until the desired length is reached.

■ If you want to make longer rows, add however many "stitches" you want by stringing on more beads to the downward side of the row (Fig. 4). For example, let's say you want the third row to be three "stitches" long instead of two. Then proceed as follows:

a. On the downward side of row 3, string on 1 green and 2 blue beads, and pass the needle back through the last green bead strung onto the upward side of the previous row.

b. String on 2 blue, 1 green, and 2 blue beads. Pass the needle back through the first green bead strung onto the upward side of the previous row.

c. String on 2 blue, 1 green, 2 blue, 1 green, 2 blue, 1 green, and 1 blue bead.

d. Now start the upward side of the row. Pass the needle back through the last green bead from the downward side of the row.

e. String on 2 blue, 1 green, and 2 blue beads, and pass the needle back through the third green bead strung onto the downward side of the row.

f. String on 2 blue, 1 green, and 2 blue beads. Pass the needle back through the second green bead strung onto the downward side of the row.

g. String on 2 blue, 1 green, and 2 blue beads. Pass the needle back through the first green bead strung on the downward side of the row.

Horizontal Netting

There are several ways to make horizontal net. One, explained here, ensures that the edges of the netting are even and that the width of the piece is consistent throughout. Another way creates rows of netting of decreasing size. For these examples we used blue and green beads in groups of 7 beads per "stitch" and made the rows only 3 "stitches" long. Any amount of beads can be used for each stitch as long as the number is odd. Groups of 3, 5, and 7 are typical numbers of beads used per stitch.

Consistent-Width Netting

To make consistent-width horizontal net, follow these instructions:

Row 1 (Fig. 1):
■ Make a knot on the end of a length of thread. Pass the needle through the edge of the fabric so that the knot is hidden in the seam. Then:

a. *String on 3 blue, 1 green, and 3 blue beads, and make a small stitch in the fabric about ¼" (6 mm) away from the place where the thread is

coming out of the fabric.* (This length will vary depending on the number and size of beads used per "stitch.") Repeat between the asterisks 2 times or however many times you need.

b. Now you will make the turn-around "stitch" (Fig. 2). String on 3 blue, 1 green, 3 blue, 1 green, and 3 blue beads. Then pass the needle back through the green bead from the third stitch of row 1.

Row 2 (Fig. 2):
a. String on 3 blue, 1 green, and 3 blue beads. Then pass the needle

back through the second green bead from row 1.

b. String on 3 blue, 1 green, and 3 blue beads. Pass the needle back through the first green bead from row 1.

c. To make the turnaround "stitch," string on 3 blue, 1 green, 3 blue, 1 green, and 3 blue beads. Pass the needle back through the green bead from the third stitch of row 2.

Remaining Rows:
■ Continue for as many rows of horizontal net as are desired.

Photo 12 is an example of horizontal netting.

1. First row of consistent-width horizontal net.

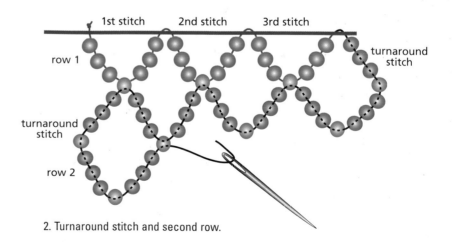

2. Turnaround stitch and second row.

Decreasing-Width Netting

■ To make the decreasing-size horizontal net, follow these instructions (Fig. 3).

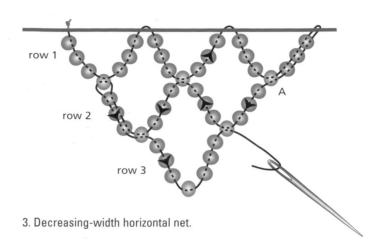

3. Decreasing-width horizontal net.

Row 1:

a. Make a knot on the end of a length of thread. Pass the needle through the edge of the fabric so the knot is hidden in the seam.

b. *String on 3 blue, 1 green, and 3 blue beads, and make a small stitch in the fabric about ¼″ (6 mm) away from the place where the original thread is coming out of the fabric.* (This length will vary depending on the number and size of beads used per "stitch.") Repeat between the asterisks 2 times, or as many times as you need.

c. Pass the needle back through the last 3 blue beads and the last green bead strung on (A).

Row 2:

a. String on 3 blue, 1 green, and 3 blue beads. Pass the needle back through the second green bead from row 1.

b. String on 3 blue, 1 green, and 3 blue beads. Pass the needle back through the first green bead from row 1. Pass the needle back through the last 3 blue beads and the last green bead you just strung on.

Row 3:

■ String on 3 blue, 1 green, and 3 blue beads, and pass the needle back through the first green bead from row 2. Pass the thread through the beads until you reach the fabric, and make a knot.

Photo 12. Horizontal netting on a denim shirt pocket.

Daisy Chain

There are many ways to make beaded daisy chains. No matter how the threads go through the beads, the outcome is the same, fun and fanciful daisy chains! The bead and color combinations are limitless. No one seems to know where or when the daisy chain was first introduced, but aren't we glad it was! In the projects in this book, the single daisy and the attached daisy are used. Use size 11° seed beads or smaller for dainty flowers, and use combinations of seed beads and larger beads or crystals for flowers with large centers. Pearls make a pretty daisy. Try stringing leaf-shaped beads in with the stem beads. Or make your own leaves with a loop of seed beads. Be creative and have fun with this easy stitch.

Photo 13. Attached daisy stitch on pants pocket.

Single Daisy

For this example, we used 8 teal beads for the petals, 1 green center bead, and 3 green beads for the stem (Fig. 1).

1. Daisy chain stitch.

1. Thread the needle, and string on 3 green beads.

2. *String on 8 teal beads. Pass the needle back through the first teal bead strung on, forming a circle (the petal beads). Pull tight and keep tight. String on 1 larger green bead (the center bead), and pass the needle back through the fifth bead strung on. String on 3 green beads for the stem.*

3. Repeat between the asterisks until the desired length is reached.

Attached Daisy

The attached daisy chain method we use in this book (Figs. 1 and 2) is only one of many. It is done as follows:

1. String on 8 teal beads, and pass the needle back through the first bead strung to form the petals.

2. String on 1 larger green bead for the center, and then pass the needle back through the fifth bead strung on.

3. *String on on 2 teal beads (the attachment beads), and then pass the needle back through the sixth and fifth beads strung on. Pass the needle back through the 2 attachment beads (Fig. 1). String on 6 teal beads. Pass the needle back through one of the attachment beads, forming a circle, and then string on a green center bead. Pass the needle back through the fourth teal bead just strung on* (Fig. 2).

Repeat between the asterisks until the desired length is attained.

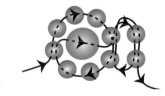

1. Adding attachment beads.

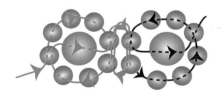

2. Making an attached daisy.

Loom Bead Weaving

Weaving beads on a loom is a fairly recent development in the bead world. The most primitive form of bead loom, a bow loom, is made with a bowed stick. The natives of North America, New Guinea, and the Amazon region of South America have all used bow looms for beadwork. The bow loom works on the premise that the force of the stick trying to unbend itself puts pressure on the warp threads, causing them to be held taut. North American natives used bow looms and suspension looms for weaving beads. On a suspension loom, one end of each of the warp threads is attached to a tree and the other to the beader's belt. Most bead weaving, past and present, uses the square weave technique, in which the warp and weft threads are straight up and down, perpendicular to each other. Occasionally bias or diagonal weave is used. Diagonal weave, which is actually a type of one-sided braiding whereby the end warp threads pass through the beads, becoming the weft threads, was used on suspension-type looms.

Southwestern Native Americans had very sophisticated looms for weaving rugs and cloth, but these were not used for beadwork. Manufactured looms made specifically for loomed bead weaving didn't arrive there until the late 1800s or early 1900s.

There are two sets of threads in loom bead weaving. The warp threads are the vertical threads attached to the loom; the weft threads run horizontally and hold the beads in place. They make special blunt-ended, 7½″ (19 cm) bead loom weaving needles. This helps with wide designs.

Warping the Loom

The first step is to attach the warp threads to the loom.

1. You need one more warp thread than there are beads in the design. For example, if the design calls for 7 beads across, you will need to attach 8 warp threads to the loom. Sometimes, for extra stability, two threads are used for each end warp instead of one thread for each end warp.

2. To calculate the length of the warp threads, add 12″ (30 cm) to the length of the finished project for tying to the loom and 12″ (30 cm) more for finishing the project.

3. There are two ways to warp a loom, depending on how long the finished project is and what kind of loom you are using.

Project Longer Than Loom

4. If the project is longer than the loom, you must cut each warp thread to the length that was calculated. When you have the desired number of warp threads cut to the desired length, tie one end of the group of warp threads to the tack or tacks on the rollers at the top of the loom.

a. Loosen the wing nuts that hold the rollers steady, and wind up the warp threads onto the roller, all the while keeping the other end of the threads tightly in hand, so that the threads stay taut. Keep rolling until there is more than enough length left to tie the threads to the other tack or tacks on the other roller.

b. Before the thread ends are tied, you must line up the threads in the coils on the springs at both the top

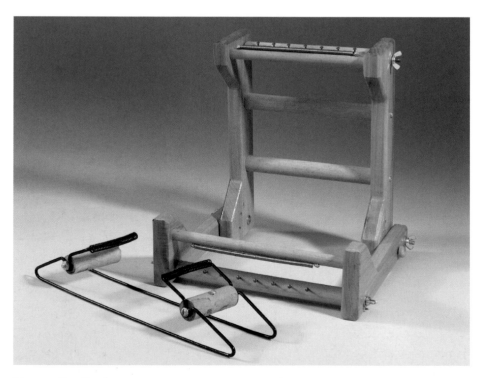

Photo 14. Beading looms.

and bottom of the loom. Now tie the threads to the other tack or tacks. Tighten the thread on the rollers, and then tighten the wing nuts.

Project Shorter Than Loom

5. If your project is shorter than the loom and there is no fringe on the project, you may want to warp the loom in a continuous fashion, as follows:

a. Make a small loop on the end of the thread still on the spool. Hook this loop around a tack on one of the rollers.

b. Calculate how many warp threads you need, and start the warp thread in a coil so the work will be centered on the loom.

c. Bring the thread down in a straight line to the corresponding coil on the other side of the loom.

d. Wrap the thread around the tack on the roller, then up through the next coil, and on up to the corresponding coil on the other side of the loom. Keep going through the coils and around the tacks, keeping an even tension on the thread, until you have the desired amount of warp threads. When you are finished, tie the thread end to the tack, and cut off the excess thread.

Weaving

Now you are ready to start weaving. We like to work from the bottom of the design and progress toward the top. When you are tying on the weft thread, make sure you leave enough space, 1″ to 2″ (2.5 to 5 cm) at the beginning of the warp threads for finishing the work.

1. With a small knot, attach about 2′ (61 cm) of weft thread to the left outermost warp thread at the bottom of the loom, leaving a

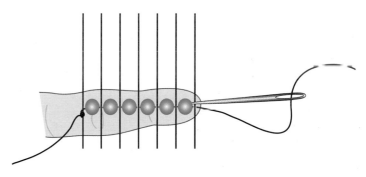

1. Push the beads up between the warp threads with your finger.

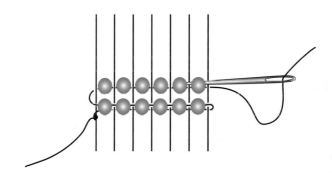

2. Make sure the needle passes through the beads over the warp threads.

6″ (15 cm) tail. Thread the beading needle to the end of the weft thread.

2. Make sure that the weft thread is under the warp threads, and string on the first row of beads, following the design chart, reading it from left to right, and bottom to top.

3. Push the beads on the weft thread up into the warp threads with your left index finger, so there is a warp thread on both sides of each bead (Fig. 1).

4. Keep your finger pressed under the beads, and pass the needle back through the beads going from right to left, making sure that the thread passes over the warp threads so the beads will be held in place.

5. String on the beads for the next row, push them into the warp

thread spaces, and pass the needle back through the beads going from right to left and making sure the thread goes over the warp threads and not under or through them (Fig. 2). Continue in this manner until you finish the design or you run out of thread.

6. When you have only about 6″ (15 cm) of weft thread left, you must start a new thread, as follows:

a. Remove the needle, and leave the 6″ (15 cm) of thread to be woven in later.

b. Thread the needle onto a new length of thread, and pass the needle through about 3 rows of beads until the needle comes out where the 6″ (15 cm) tail is. Then continue weaving with the new thread.

Finishing Loomwork

There are several ways to finish a piece of loomwork. Here are two ways to do it.

1. If the project doesn't really have a back side, and both sides must look like they are the front of the work, then you finish it as follows:

a. Remove the work from the loom a few warp threads at a time.

b. Using the beading needle, pass each warp thread through several rows of beading. It helps to use a thinner beading needle, like a size 12, so you can pass more threads through each bead. Make sure you don't pack the beads too full of thread or they might break.

Photo 15. Closeup of loomed orchid design.

c. When the beads become full, instead of weaving the warp threads through the beads, weave them back up the warp threads (Fig. 3).

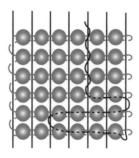

3. Weaving in warp thread ends.

2. If there is a back side to the work, finish it as follows:

a. Weave about ⅜″ (1 cm) of thread cloth to hold the beads tightly onto the warp threads. To do this, *use the weft thread without any beads on it. Go over and under and over and under the warp threads until you reach the end of the row. For the next row, go under and over and under and over until you reach the end of the row.*

b. Repeat between the asterisks for several more rows until you have the desired length of thread cloth (Fig. 4).

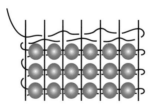

4. Weaving the thread cloth at the end of the project.

c. Every row or two, make sure you beat down the weft threads so they are up against the beads. You may use a comb if you wish.

d. Next make a ⅜″ (1 cm) thread cloth on the other side of the work. Tie a new weft thread, and repeat between the asterisks until you have the desired length of thread cloth.

e. Remove the piece from the loom, and tie off all pairs of warp threads with square knots. Cut the excess thread, and fold the thread cloths to the back of the work. If necessary, glue in place.

Decreasing Loomwork

1. To decrease at the beginning of the row, proceed as follows:

a. Before going back through the beads, pass the weft thread under the outermost warp thread.

b. Pass the needle back through the number of beads to be decreased, and start the next row at this point (Fig. 5).

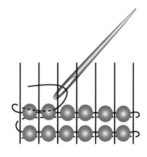

5. Decreasing at the beginning of the row.

2. To decrease at the end of the row, string on the new amount of beads (less the decreased number of beads), and pass the needle back through the beads as usual, ignoring the excess warp threads (Fig. 6).

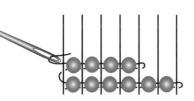

6. Decreasing at the end of the row.

Beaded Needle Tatting

Photo 16. Beaded needle-tatted design has beads on picots.

Tatting is a form of lace-making that uses a needle, a shuttle, or the bare hand. It seems that both needle and shuttle tatting have been around for about 200 years. Early tatting consisted only of rings and was made in small sections, which were painstakingly sewn together after they were tatted. Mademoiselle Riego de la Brachardière, a lace-making and embroidery supply shop owner in London in the mid-1800s, popularized tatting with her instructional tatting books. She invented a way to join the small sections with a netting needle while tatting. It wasn't until the beginning of the 20th century that a book by Lady Katherine Hoare popularized the chain, which made joining the rings easier.

Shuttle tatting is more widely used than needle tatting, probably because in the 1800s, elaborate and beautifully made shuttles were almost a status symbol and looked prettier in the hands than a needle. Tatting is basically a series of lark's head knots tied on a thread. These knots are formed into rings and chains. There are two methods of needle tatting: the ring-and-thread method worked with a thread cut from the ball, and the ring-and-chain method worked off the ball. To work off the ball means that the beads are strung onto the ball of thread and the thread is not cut from the ball. In needle tatting, the stitches are formed around the needle and then pushed down onto the thread. In shuttle tatting, the stitches are formed directly around the thread.

All the tatting projects in this book are needle-tatted, using the ring-and-chain method. They are worked off the ball and use beads in the picots only. Picots are decorative loops of thread, with or without beads on them, added between the double stitches to rings or chains. They stick up above the double stitches.

Beads can be added to tatting in the picots, on the thread in the ring-and-thread method, and/or in between the half-stitches of the double stitch. For tatting, you can use a variety of threads. Be creative, and don't think you have to tat exclusively with cotton crochet thread; it all depends on the look you want to achieve. Use silk, metallic embroidery braid, or velour thread; there are many possibilities, as long as the beads fit the thread.

Beaded Needle Tatting Worked Off the Ball: Ring-and-Chain Method

Ring

To make a ring with beaded picots, work as follows:

1. Use a twisted beading needle to string the desired number and color or colors of beads onto the ball of thread. Remove the twisted needle, and thread on the tatting needle, leaving about a 4″ (10 cm) tail. Keep the ball of thread to your left when tatting.

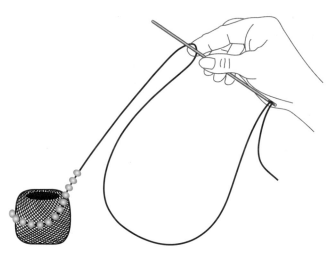

1. Holding the tatting thread in place, ready to begin tatting.

2. Wrapping the thread around your left index finger.

2. Hold the thread with your right index finger on the side of the needle, which is facing away from you, holding it about three-fourths of the way up the needle. Leave a loop of thread anywhere from 20″ (51 cm) to 2 yd (183 cm), depending on the size of the project, between the eye of the needle and the place where you start tatting (Fig. 1). This loop of thread is what the knots are slipped onto.

a. Take the thread coming from the ball in your left hand, and wrap the thread around your left index finger over the top and clockwise (Fig. 2).

b. Pass the needle under the thread on your left index finger, and bring the loop of thread off your finger and onto the needle (Fig. 3).

c. Pull the thread tight, and then hold the loop securely on the needle

with your right index finger. This forms the first half of the double stitch.

3. Wrap the thread coming from the ball around your left index finger counterclockwise. Then bend your finger (Fig. 4) and pass the needle under the thread on your left index finger in the direction from the knuckle to the fingertip (Fig. 5).

b. Bring the loop of thread off your finger and onto the needle. This completes the double stitch

3. Bringing the loop of thread off your finger onto the needle.

(Fig. 6). For this example, make 3 double stitches.

4. To make a beaded picot, push the desired number of beads (5 for this example) up to the needle, and then make a double stitch (Fig. 7).

a. Push the double stitch up against the other double stitches.

b. Make as many picots and double stitches as desired, and then form the ring.

c. Beaded picots that will be used as the join should have an even

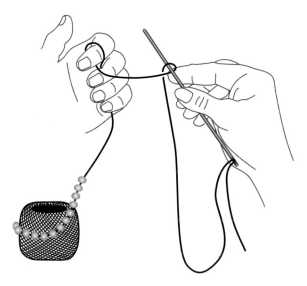

4. Bending your finger so you can pass the needle under the thread.

number of beads (4 in this example), and decorative picots should have an odd number of beads (5 in this example).

d. To make a picot without beads, leave a length of thread about ¼" (6 mm) after the last double stitch, and hold it in place on the needle with your right index finger. Now make a double stitch, leaving the ¼" (6 mm) space, and continue according to your pattern.

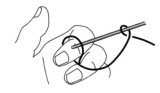

5. Passing the needle under the thread on your finger.

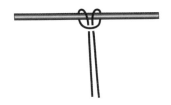

6. Double stitch.

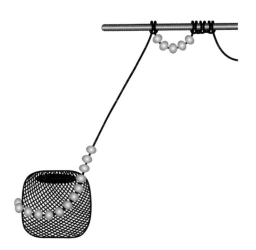

7. Making a beaded picot.

5. To form the ring or "close the ring," grab the double stitches with your left hand and the tip of the needle with your right hand (Fig. 8).

a. While still holding the double stitches, pull the needle until the double stitches have passed the eye of the needle and slipped onto the thread.

b. Keep pulling on the needle until the thread forms a small loop. (Don't pull too fast or the loop might be pulled into the stitches and you will make a chain instead of a ring.) Then pass the needle up through this loop (Fig. 9). Pull tight until a ring is formed (Fig. 10).

6. Now reverse the work (rw), as follows:

a. Flip the ring right over left, like turning a book page. The wrong side of the tatting will now face toward you. This will cross the ball and needle threads, forming a small teardrop space.

b. Pass the needle up through this space, and pull both threads tight. This is an overhand knot. Keep the wrong side of the tatting facing toward you, and then you are ready to make a chain. To tell the difference between the right side and the wrong side, look at the thread of a picot, and follow it to the double stitches. If the thread is smooth, it is the wrong side; if you see the bumps of the double stitches over the picot, it is the right side.

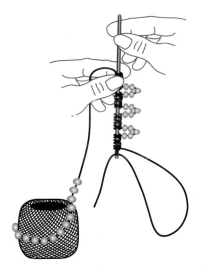

8. Push the stitches down the needle and onto the thread.

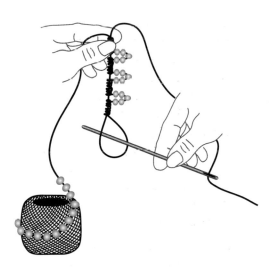

9. Pass the needle through the loop.

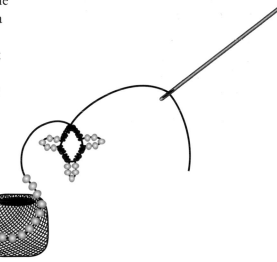

10. Pull tight to form a ring.

Chain

To make a chain with beaded picots (Fig. 11), work as follows:

7. Place the needle on top of the ring, perpendicular to the closure. Then make a double stitch right next to the ring. Make as many double stitches and picots as desired.

8. Grab the double stitches with your left hand and the tip of the needle with your right hand, and then pull the needle until the double stitches have passed the eye of the needle and slipped onto the thread. Keep pulling until the thread connected to the needle disappears into the double stitches.

9. Now reverse the work, as follows:

a. Flip the chain and the ring right over left. The wrong side of the chain will now face toward you. This will cross the threads, forming a small teardrop-shaped space.

b. Pass the needle up through this space, and pull both threads tight. This is an overhand knot. Keep the wrong side of the chain facing toward you, and then you are ready to make the second ring.

10. The second ring must be joined to the first ring by the picots, as follows:

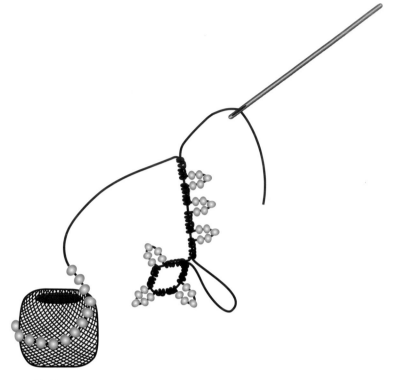

11. Making a chain with beaded picots.

a. Place the needle on top of the chain with the tip of the needle facing the same direction as the half-square knot just made.

b. Make the number of double stitches desired, and then, instead of making a picot, place the thread under the picot to be joined (usually the last picot made on the previous ring).

c. Using the needle (or, if you prefer, a small crochet hook), pull the thread up and out of the picot.

d. Slip this loop of thread onto the needle, and pull tight so the joined picot is right next to the needle. This loop on the thread is not part of the double stitches; it is the join loop.

e. Then make the desired number of double stitches and picots and close the ring as in Step 5.

Common Tatting Abbreviations

Common abbreviations used in tatting are as follows. Figure 12 explains the charting symbols used in tatting patterns.

r = ring
ds = double stitch
cl = close
rw = reverse the work
j = join
p = picot

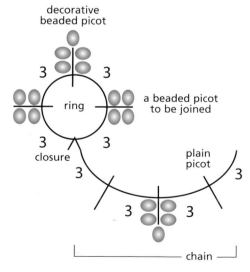

12. Diagram showing charting symbols used in tatting patterns. Numeral (here 3) shows number of double stitches to make between picots.

General Beading Tips

■ Stretch the thread before you use it, to remove the kinks. The straighter the thread, the less it knots and tangles. When you pull the thread tight it is stretched, which erases the memory of being rolled onto a spool.

■ Never use pencil when marking on fabric (it doesn't come off), and never use pencil when tracing the pattern onto the tracing paper. When the needle punctures the tracing paper, small amounts of graphite are deposited, which discolor the fabric. Use fabric markers that are specially made for easy removal from the fabric.

■ When removing stubborn pieces of tracing paper from under the beads after using the trace-and-baste transfer method, a sharp diagonal or needle nose tweezers is very helpful.

■ When embroidering on already made clothing, it is sometimes hard to use a hoop because of the size and shape of the clothing. If you are more comfortable using a hoop, there are ways to use one even if the hoop is too large or too small for the garment to be beaded. Cut out a piece of cotton fabric so that it fits nicely in your hoop, and then cut a circle out of the middle of the fabric. Pin the article to be beaded under the hoop onto the cotton fabric, with the area to be covered in beads showing through the hole. When you pin the article onto the cotton fabric, make sure you pull the article as tight as you can.

■ Before you glue beads onto an object, make sure the beads are colorfast. The dye in certain dyed beads will run into the glue, discoloring the object and the beads.

■ A good knot to use when ending a body of work is the very secure double overhand knot. Make a loop in the thread, then stick the needle into the loop, and twist the needle around the thread so the thread is looped around the needle. Twist the needle around the thread one more time so there are two thread loops on the needle. Then pull the needle through the two loops, and pull tight.

■ When using a stitch that requires the thread to go through each bead repeatedly, it is a good idea to use a smaller beading needle (for instance, a size 13) and a smaller size thread, so if there is a pesky bead with an extra small hole, the needle will still go through without breaking the bead. This is especially true with size 11° or 15° seed beads.

■ When couching, use a long beading needle for the beaded thread and a short beading needle for the thread used to tack down the beaded thread. This makes it easy to distinguish between the two threads.

■ Always buy more beads than called for or you think you'll need, just in case. It is so much better to have leftover beads than to run out and have to buy more of the same beads before you can finish the project. Sometimes it is hard to find the bead again, even at the same bead shop. Besides, leftover beads are always handy to have around. Bead sizes vary, and the same technique done by different people will sometimes require more or fewer beads.

■ Always have plenty of beading needles handy, especially when working with leather or heavy fabric. Bead needles break easily. Use a pliers or a square of leather to help pull the needle through the leather or fabric. You might want to use short beading needles as they don't break as easily as the longer ones.

■ Bugle beads often have very sharp edges and can cut the beading thread. You might want to sand the edges of the bugle beads with a fine grit sandpaper before use. You can also place seed beads at either end of the bugle bead.

■ When tatting with beads, use an even number of beads in a joining picot and an odd number of beads in a decorative picot.

■ Japanese tubular beads (Delica beads) are the best kind of seed beads to use for loom work because of their consistent size and shape and large holes. The seed beads used in loomwork must be consistent or the work will be uneven (Photo 17).

Photo 17. Delica beads.

■ It is a good idea to launder an article of clothing that you will be beading before you begin, so it will be preshrunk and won't pucker your beadwork.

■ You can check your beads for color permanence by performing a few easy experiments. Leave a few beads in direct sunlight for several days. Sand the outside of the beads and see whether the color peels off. Put several beads on a thread, and rub them back and forth to see whether the color on the inside of the bead comes off. Put the beads in nail polish remover, bleach, or rubbing alcohol and see what happens. Sew a few beads onto a piece of fabric, wash it in the washing machine, and then put it in the dryer. Try dry cleaning the piece of beaded fabric. If your beads pass these tests, they should stay as good as new for many years.

■ If the embroidery hoop diameter is smaller than the beaded area, sooner or later you must put a section of already beaded fabric in between the two hoops. Glue strips of felt on the inside of both hoops.

Photo 18. Crochet threads.

Photo 19. Closeup of bead-embroidered necklace with accent beads.

This will protect the beads and hold the fabric in place so you won't have to make the outer hoop fit too tightly. You might want to do this even if the beads won't have to be fitted in between the hoop.

■ A good light source is essential for doing close work such as beadwork.

■ When embroidering with beads, make sure you leave enough space between the stitches, or the beads will not lie flat and the fabric below will be distorted. With a little practice, the correct spacing of the stitches will become second nature.

■ When you can, do your beadwork on a piece of separate material and make an appliqué, so you can move your beadwork from shirts, to pants, to hats, etc. You can also take the beadwork off for laundering.

■ When laundering an article of clothing with beads on it, it is a good idea to put the garment into a pillowcase for protection. (Tie the end closed, so the garment won't come out of the pillowcase in the wash.) Wash with cold water on the gentle cycle. Also, when ironing a

beaded garment, try to iron around the beaded area unless most of the garment is beaded. In that case, turn the garment inside out so the beads are facing the ironing board, and place a towel between the garment and the iron to protect the beads and beading thread from the heat and the pressure of the iron.

■ There are approximately 17 size 6° seed beads per gram, approximately 115 size 11° seed beads per gram, and approximately 195 Delica beads per gram.

■ If you buy your thread in bulk and you don't want to carry around a large spool of thread, simply use a sewing machine and from the large spool make a small one on a bobbin.

■ If you don't have a twisted beading needle or a big-eye needle handy and you have to put your beads on thread that won't go through the eye of the beading needle, you can make a big "eye" for your needle with very thin beading thread such as Nymo™ nylon monofilament size 00. Thread your needle with about a 6″ (15 cm) length of Nymo size 00 thread. Tie the two ends together with a small knot, making a small loop about ½″ (1 cm) long, and cut off excess thread ends. This loop forms the new larger "eye." Now thread your thick thread through this loop and you are ready to string beads.

■ When bead looming, so as not to catch the warp threads and split them, you can cut off the very tip of the beading needle with wire cutters and then file down the rough edges.

■ If you don't have a light box, you can use a window to transfer a design onto thin, light-colored fabric for use in a bead appliqué. Tape the fabric to the window over the design, and trace around the design with a fabric marker.

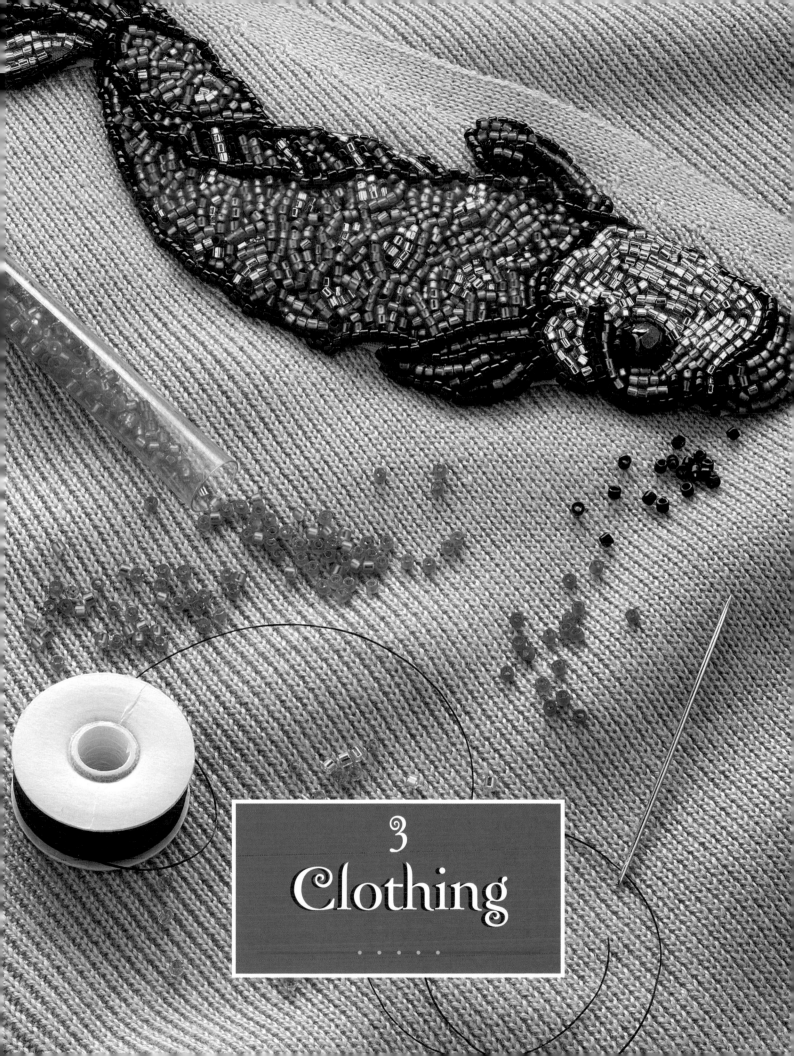

3
Clothing

Tatted T-Shirt

Cotton is generally planted at the start of the summer, and about two months later, the plant flowers. The cotton plant has grown wild around the world for millions of years, and cotton has been made into cloth for thousands of years. In Mexico, pieces of cotton cloth and cotton bolls (seed pods) 7000 years old were found in a cave; 5000-year-old pieces of cotton cloth have been found in Pakistan. This cotton T-shirt is embellished with bead tatting and bead zipper-stitch edging. The tatted edging would look pretty on a blouse or scarf as well.

MATERIALS

Pale green size 11° Japanese seed beads, 10 g

Twisted wire beading needle, medium size

Tatting needle, size 5

Ball of spruce color crochet thread, size 10

Embroidery needle

Beading needle, size 11

Black or green Nymo nylon mono-filament beading thread, size D

Blue cotton T-shirt, or any color you like

Neck Edge

1. Using the twisted beading needle, string 72″ (183 cm) of green beads onto the thread ball. There will be approximately 16 beads per inch (6 per cm). Remove the twisted needle, and thread on the tatting needle, leaving a 4″ (10 cm) tail.

2. See section on beaded needle tatting in Chapter 2 for general instructions. Start tatting about 1 yd (1 m) from the needle as follows:

a. To make the first ring (Fig. 1), follow this pattern: 3 double stitches, 8-bead picot, 5 double stitches, 8-bead picot, 3 double stitches; then close the ring (cl) and reverse the work (rw).

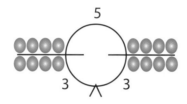

1. First bead-tatted ring; 3, 5, and 3 are the groups of double stitches.

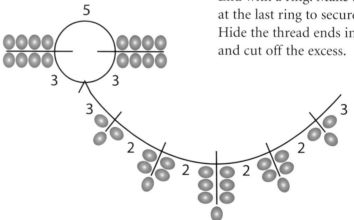

2. Bead-tatted chain, working from the ring to the right.

b. To make the chain (Fig. 2), follow this pattern: 3 double stitches, 3-bead picot, 2 double stitches, 5-bead picot, 2 double stitches, 7-bead picot, 2 double stitches, 5-bead picot, 2 double stitches, 3-bead picot, 3 double stitches; then close the ring and reverse the work.

c. The second ring follows this pattern: 3 double stitches, join (J) to the second 8-bead picot on the previous ring. Then do 5 double stitches, 8-bead picot, 3 double stitches; then cl and rw (close the ring and reverse the work).

d. Repeat this tatting pattern until you have 21 rings or until you have made enough tatting to go around the neck opening of your T-shirt. End with a ring. Make a square knot at the last ring to secure the tatting. Hide the thread ends in the work, and cut off the excess.

Closeup of neck edge.

3. Using the embroidery needle and beading thread, sew the tatting to the front of the T-shirt all along the neckline.

Sleeves

4. To make the zipper-stitch edging along the bottom of the sleeves, use the beading needle and about 3 yd (274 cm) of beading thread:

a. Tie a knot on the end of the thread, and pass the needle through the hem of the sleeve near the seam (to hide the knot).

b. Bring the needle out of the fabric, and string on 3 green beads.

c. Make a small stitch on the edge of the sleeve about ⅛″ (3 mm) from the place where the thread is coming out of the fabric, and pass the needle back through the third bead strung on (Fig. 3).

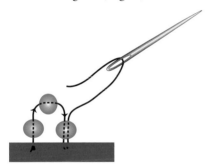

3. First stitch of the zipper-stitch edging along the bottom of the sleeves.

d. String on 2 beads (Fig. 4). Make a small stitch in the fabric about ⅛″ (3 mm) from the place where the thread is coming out of the fabric, and pass the needle back through the last bead strung on (Fig. 5).

e. Repeat this stitch all around the edge of the sleeve.

f. On the last stitch, string on only 1 bead, and then pass the needle through the first bead from the very first stitch. Tie a small knot, and then pass the needle through the

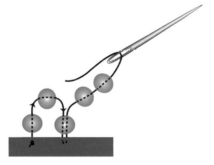

4. String 2 green beads for the 2nd stitch.

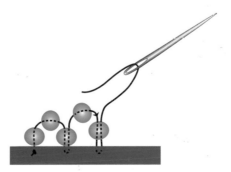

5. Make a small stitch in the fabric, and pass the needle back through the last bead.

hem of the sleeve. Make another knot, and hide the thread end in the hem. Cut off the excess thread.

5. Repeat Step 4 to edge the other sleeve.

Closeup of sleeve edge.

Plaid Net T-Shirt

Named after its shape, the T-shirt became popular with the troops in World War I as an article of comfortable underwear. It wasn't until the 1950s that the T-shirt was accepted as outerwear. Printing and dyeing of T-shirts began in the 1960s, and such shirts are now American icons. Inspired by the fabric-like quality of vertical netting, we decided to make sleeves out of beads. Bead "fabric" has a fluidity that cannot be rivaled. Netting like this would be pretty on a sleeveless dress as well.

MATERIALS

Size 11° seed beads, 15 g of each of the following: opaque yellow; opaque orange; transparent turquoise lined; transparent green lined; transparent red lined

Beading needle, size 11 or 12 (pick a size that best fits the bead holes)

White Nymo nylon monofilament beading thread, size D

Embroidery scissors

Sleeveless red T-shirt (or other color)

1. Make the base strand for the vertical net sleeve cap as follows. I used lots of thread for this project, because I hate changing thread in the middle of a piece.

a. Thread the needle with about 6 yd (548 cm) of thread, and place a stop bead on one end. A stop bead is a bead that is temporarily tied to the end of the thread to keep the other beads from falling off.

b. String on *1 yellow, 1 turquoise, 1 green, 1 yellow, 1 green, 1 turquoise, 1 yellow, 1 orange, 1 red, 1 yellow, 1 red, and 1 orange bead.* Repeat between the asterisks 11 times until you have 144 beads. (This amount may have to be adjusted to fit the top of the armhole on the shirt used.)

c. String on 1 yellow, 1 turquoise, 1 green, 1 yellow, 1 green, 1 turquoise, 1 yellow, 1 orange, 1 red, and 1 yellow bead. The base strand is finished.

Note: When stringing the base strand for the second sleeve, don't be alarmed if it seems too short. As the vertical net stitch is worked, it will expand the strand to be the same length as the first one.

2. To position the needle for the first row, skip the last yellow bead strung on, and then pass the needle back through the last red, orange, and yellow beads strung on the base strand (Fig. 1).

a. Downward side of row 1 (Fig. 2): String on 1 yellow, 1 orange, 1 red, 1 yellow, 1 red, 1 orange, 1 yellow, 1 turquoise, 1 green, 1 yellow, 1 green, and 1 turquoise bead. Pass

the needle back through the third yellow bead strung on the downward side of the row.

b. Upward side of row 1: String on 1 orange, 1 red, 1 yellow, 1 red, and 1 orange bead, and then pass the needle back through the first yellow bead from the downward side of row 1.

3. To finish off the end of the base strand (Fig. 3), pass the needle back through the first yellow, orange, red, and yellow beads on the base strand. Then string on 1 yellow, 1 turquoise, and 1 green bead. Pass the needle back through the second yellow bead strung on the downward side of row 1. Then pass the needle back through the beads on the downward and upward sides so the needle is coming out of the top of the first yellow bead strung on the downward side of the first row.

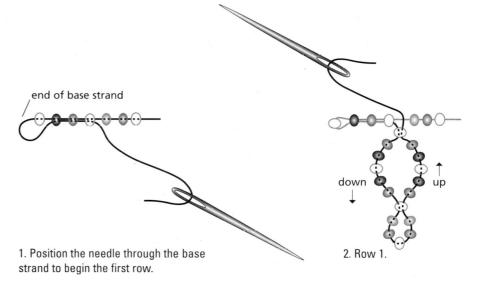

end of base strand

1. Position the needle through the base strand to begin the first row.

down ↓   up ↑

2. Row 1.

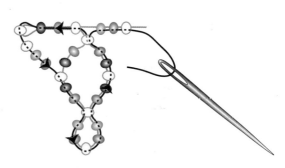

3. Finishing off the end.

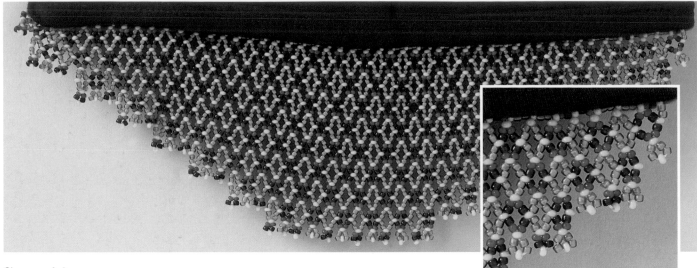

Closeup of sleeve.

4. Make row 2 as follows:

a. Downward side of row 2 (Fig. 4): Pass the needle through the next turquoise, green, and yellow bead to the right on the base strand. String on 1 yellow, 1 turquoise, and 1 green bead. Then pass the needle through the second yellow bead on the upward side of row 1. String on 1 green, 1 turquoise, 1 yellow, 1 orange, 1 red, 1 yellow, 1 red, 1 orange, 1 yellow, 1 turquoise, 1 green, 1 yellow, 1 green, and 1 turquoise bead. Pass the needle back through the fourth yellow bead strung on the downward side of the row.

b. Upward side of row 2 (Fig. 4): String on 1 orange, 1 red, 1 yellow, 1 red, and 1 orange bead. Then pass

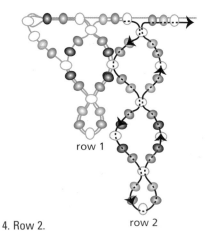

4. Row 2.

the needle back through the second yellow bead strung on the downward side of the row. String on 1 turquoise, 1 green, 1 yellow, 1 green, and 1 turquoise bead. Pass the needle back through the first yellow bead strung on the downward side of the row (Fig. 4). Pass the needle back through the next green, turquoise, and yellow beads on the base strand. Now the needle is properly positioned for row 3.

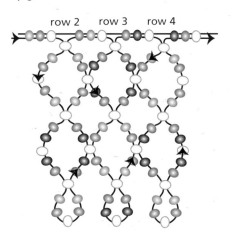

5. Rows 2, 3, and 4, showing alternating colors.

5. Repeat row 2 two more times to make rows 3 and 4. Make sure to alternate the "stitch" colors (Fig. 5).

6. Make the rest of the rows as follows, remembering to alternate the colors of each row:

Rows 5 to 7: Three stitches long

Rows 8 to 10: Four stitches long

Rows 11 to 13: Five stitches long

Rows 14 to 16: Six stitches long

Rows 17 to 19: Seven stitches long

Rows 20 to 31: Eight stitches long

Rows 32 to 34: Seven stitches long

Rows 35 to 37: Six stitches long

Rows 38 to 40: Five stitches long

Rows 41 to 43: Four stitches long

Rows 44 to 46: Three stitches long

Rows 47 to 49: Two stitches long

Row 50: One stitch long

7. Finish off the edge as in Step 3. Then tie off the thread, and weave the end into the beads until they are secure. Repeat Steps 1 through 7 for the other sleeve.

8. Sew one sleeve on the inside of one armhole using the running stitch and matching the middle of the bead sleeve to the center top of the armhole. Make a stitch on the inside of the armhole, and then pass the needle through the next 3 or 4 beads of the base strand. Keep sewing in this manner until done. Repeat for the other sleeve.

Horizontal Net Denim Shirt

Denim has been around for more than 400 years. Originally used for work clothes because of its durability, denim has become a favorite fabric for casual clothes and formal wear. Denim is a twill weave fabric made from cotton yarn with dyed warp threads and undyed weft threads. Indigo blue is the most popular color for denim. Before the 1870s, when synthetic indigo dye was invented by Adolf von Baeyer, indigo dye was made from the Indigofera tinctoria plant, which is native to India and

Asia, as well as the Indigofera suffruticosa, which is native to Central and South America. The leaves are placed in vats of water, where they are left to ferment. The indigo sinks to the bottom of the vat, and the water is drained off. The indigo sediment is then dried and formed into small cubes for ease of exportation. The beaded horizontal net edging gives this denim work shirt a little pizzazz. The edging could decorate a dress shirt and many other garments as well.

MATERIALS

Size 15° seed beads, 7 g each of the following: gold-lined transparent amber; teal matte; teal-lined; light blue transparent luster
Beading needle, size 12
Black Nymo nylon monofilament beading thread, size B
Denim shirt

Pocket

Row 1. Thread the needle with about 1½ yd (137 cm) of thread. Make a knot in the end, and hide it in the seam on one end of the flap of one of the pockets. Pass the needle through the fabric so it comes out along the edge of the flap. Then:

a. *String on 1 light blue, 1 teal-lined, 1 teal, 1 gold, 1 teal, 1 teal-lined, and 1 light blue bead. Pass the needle back through the fabric at a point about ³⁄₁₆″ (5 mm) away, and make a small stitch* (Fig. 1).

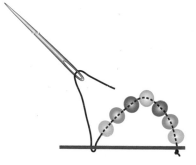

1. First horizontal net stitch and a small stitch made in the fabric.

b. Repeat between the asterisks all along the pocket flap edge. When you reach the end, after you make the last small stitch in the fabric, pass the needle back through the last light blue, teal-lined, teal, and gold beads strung on (Fig. 2).

Closeup of pocket.

Row 2. **String on 1 light blue, 1 teal-lined, 1 teal, 1 gold, 1 teal, 1 teal-lined, and 1 light blue bead. Pass the needle through the next gold bead from row 1.** Then:

a. Repeat between the double asterisks until you reach the end of row 1 (Fig. 2).

b. Pass needle back through the last light blue, teal-lined, teal, and gold beads strung on (Fig. 3).

Row 3. ***String on 5 gold beads, and pass the needle through the next gold bead on row 2.*** Then:

a. Repeat between the triple asterisks until you reach the end. Then pass the needle through the teal, teal-lined, and light blue beads on the end of row 2 and the gold, teal, teal-lined, and light blue beads on the end of row 1.

b. Make a knot, hide the thread end in between the fabric, and cut off the excess thread.

■ Repeat Rows 1 to 3 on the other pocket flap and along the edges of the collar.

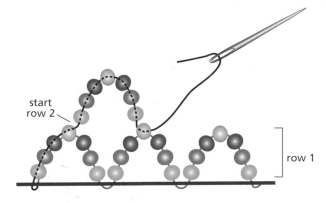

2. Start of the second row.

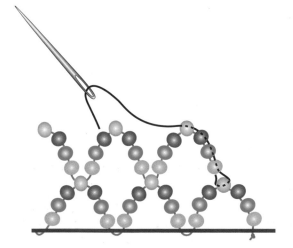

3. Bring the thread back through the beads to begin the third row.

Closeup of collar.

Daisy Chain Netted Linen Jacket

The oldest fabric known to humans is linen, which is made from flax fibers. Flax is ready to be harvested after a short growing period of 90 to 120 days. It cannot be cut when harvested, but must be pulled from the ground, roots and all, and prepared in several stages before the fibers are bleached, dyed, and are ready for spinning into cloth. This linen jacket is enhanced by beautiful daisy chain netting.

MATERIALS*

Black size 11° seed beads, 15 g

Burnt sienna AB (aurora borealis) size 6° seed beads, 20 g

Transparent gray white-heart size 11° seed beads, 10 g

Black Nymo nylon monofilament beading thread, size D

Beading needle, size 11

Light-colored erasable fabric marker

Maroon linen three-quarter sleeve jacket with a front pocket*

*Note: Use any cloth jacket you want to decorate, and adapt the bead colors to go with your jacket.

Pocket Flap and Sleeves

■ With the fabric marker, make a mark every ½″ (1 cm) all along the edge of the pocket flap. Thread a 1 yd (1 m) length of beading thread through the needle, and tie a knot on the end. Pass the needle through the seam (to hide the knot) on the edge of one side of the pocket flap.

Row 1. *String on 5 black and 10 gray beads. Pass the needle back through the first gray bead strung on. Then string on 1 burnt sienna bead, and pass the needle back through the 7th, 8th, 9th, 10th, and 1st gray beads strung on (Fig. 1). Then string on 5 black seed beads. Make a small stitch at the first ½″ (1 cm) mark (Fig. 2).* Repeat between the asterisks 8 times or until you reach the other end of the flap to complete row 1.

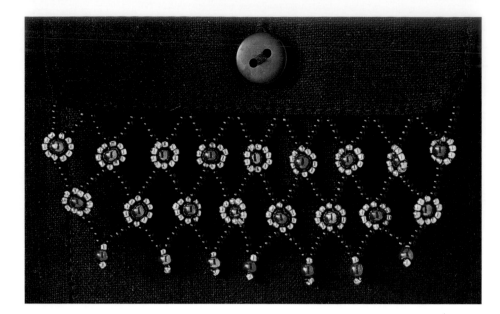

Closeup of pocket flap.

1. The daisy of the daisy chain netting stitch.

2. Finishing the daisy chain netting stitch.

Row 2 (see Fig. 3). Pass the needle back through the last 5 black beads strung on row 1 and back through the 10th, 9th, 8th, 7th, and 6th gray beads strung on the last daisy from row 1. Then:

a. *String on 5 black and 10 gray beads, and pass the needle back through the first gray bead strung on. Then string on 1 burnt sienna bead, and pass the needle back through the 7th, 8th, 9th, 10th, and 1st gray beads strung on. String on 5 black seed beads, and then pass the needle back through the top gray bead of the next daisy from row 1* (Fig. 3).

b. Repeat between the asterisks 7 times or until you reach the end of the row.

Row 3. Pass the needle back through the last 5 black beads strung on row 2 and back through the 10th, 9th, 8th, 7th, and 6th beads strung on the last daisy from row 2. Then:

a. *String on 5 black, 1 gray, 1 burnt sienna, and 1 gray bead. Pass the needle back through the burnt

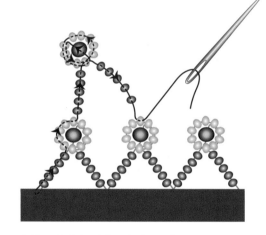

3. Row 2 of the daisy chain netting.

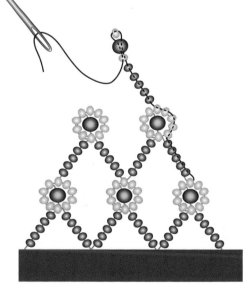

4. The start of row 3.

sienna bead and the 1st gray bead (Fig. 4). String on 5 black beads, and then pass the needle back through the top gray bead of the next daisy from row 2.*

b. Repeat between the asterisks until the end of the row.

c. Pass the needle back through several beads and daisies until the needle is back to the fabric. Make a small knot in the seam of the flap. Hide the thread end in the hem of the flap, and cut off the excess thread.

■ Repeat Rows 1 to 3 for both sleeves.

Edge of Jacket

■ To make the edging on the front buttonhole edge of the jacket, make a mark every ½″ (1 cm) all along the edge of the jacket. Then:

a. Thread a 1 yd (1 m) length of beading thread, and tie a knot on the end. Hide the knot in the hem of the jacket front, and bring the needle out of the edge at the first ½″ (1 cm) mark.

b. *String on 5 black, 1 gray, 1 burnt sienna, and 1 gray bead. Pass the needle back through the burnt sienna bead and the 1st gray bead (Fig. 5). String on 5 black beads, and then make a small stitch in the cloth edge at the next ½″ (1 cm) mark* (Fig. 6).

c. Repeat between the asterisks as many times as it takes to reach the lower end of your jacket front. Make a small knot in the seam of the jacket front. Hide the excess thread in the hem, and cut off.

5. The first half of the edging stitch along the jacket front.

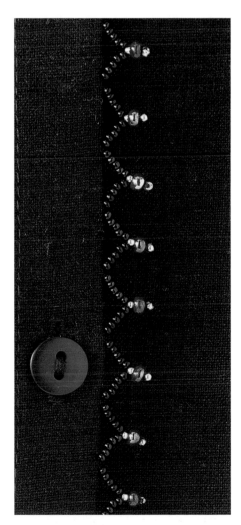

Closeup of jacket edge.

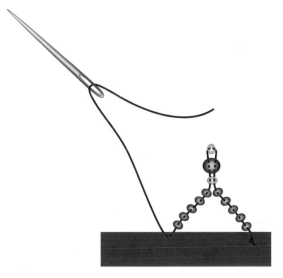

6. The edging stitch.

Koi Cardigan

Koi add graceful beauty to any pond. They are sometimes referred to as living jewels or swimming flowers. Japan is renowned for the beautiful Koi bred there. Koi were developed from carp (Cyprinus carpio) and were first introduced to Japan from China around 200 AD. They were originally used for food, but by the early 1800s in the Niigata region of Japan, they were being bred for color and beauty. The couched Koi in this project is made as an appliqué for easy removal when laundering and for moving it to another article of clothing.

MATERIALS

Delica beads as follows:
- Silver-lined gold cut, 5 g
- Silver-lined squash semi-matte, 5 g
- Silver-lined orange semi-matte, 7
- Black, 7 g

Black glass faceted 6 mm bead for the eye

Beading needle, size 11

Beading needle (short), size 11

Black Nymo nylon monofilament beading thread, size D

Spool of thread the same color as the cardigan

10" (25 cm) embroidery hoop

12" (30 cm) square of white muslin for embroidery

Tracing paper

Erasable fabric marker

Beige V-neck cardigan, or other color

Permanent flexible clear fabric glue

1. See Chapter 1 for instructions on how to transfer designs and Chapter 2 for how to couch. Trace the design (Fig. 1) onto the square of muslin using your favorite transfer technique. Stretch fabric into the embroidery hoop.

2. The long needle will hold the beaded thread. The short one will tack it onto the fabric. Thread each needle with about 3 yd (274 cm) of thread. Tie knots on the ends of both threads, and pass the long needle up through the fabric at a point along the black outline of the design. Then:

a. String on about 3" (8 cm) of black Delica beads. Push 2, 3, or 4 beads down to the fabric, depending on the straightness of the line. Use more beads for straighter lines and fewer for curves. (To ensure that all the beads lie flat, you may want to couch between every bead.)

b. Pass the short needle up through the fabric at a point along the outline that will bring the needle over the beaded thread right next to the last bead pushed down. Pass the needle back through the fabric, catching the beaded thread (Fig. 2).

c. Push more beads down on the beaded thread. Then pass the short needle back up through the fabric, over the beaded thread, and back down through the fabric. Continue couching around the black outline of the fish with the black beads.

d. To end a line of beads, string on one bead and then bring the beaded thread down through the fabric. If you don't have much thread left, tie a knot in the beaded thread and cut off the excess. If you have enough thread, bring the beaded thread back up through the fabric to the beginning of a new line in the design.

3. Outline the fish scales using the couching technique (the orange lines on the design are the outlines) with orange beads, and then fill in the scales using squash beads and gold beads. Fill in the head with gold beads, and then fill in the area under the eye and the mouth with squash beads. Check the photo for directions of the lines and bead colors. Fill in the pectoral fins with orange beads, the dorsal fin with orange and gold beads, and the tail fin with orange, gold, and squash beads.

4. Sew the 6 mm faceted bead into the black eye circle using the single stitch.

5. Remove fabric from hoop, and trim the fabric to ¼" (6 mm) around the beadwork. Glue fabric edges down to the back of the work. Let dry.

6. Sew the beadwork to the right side of the cardigan with blindstitch.

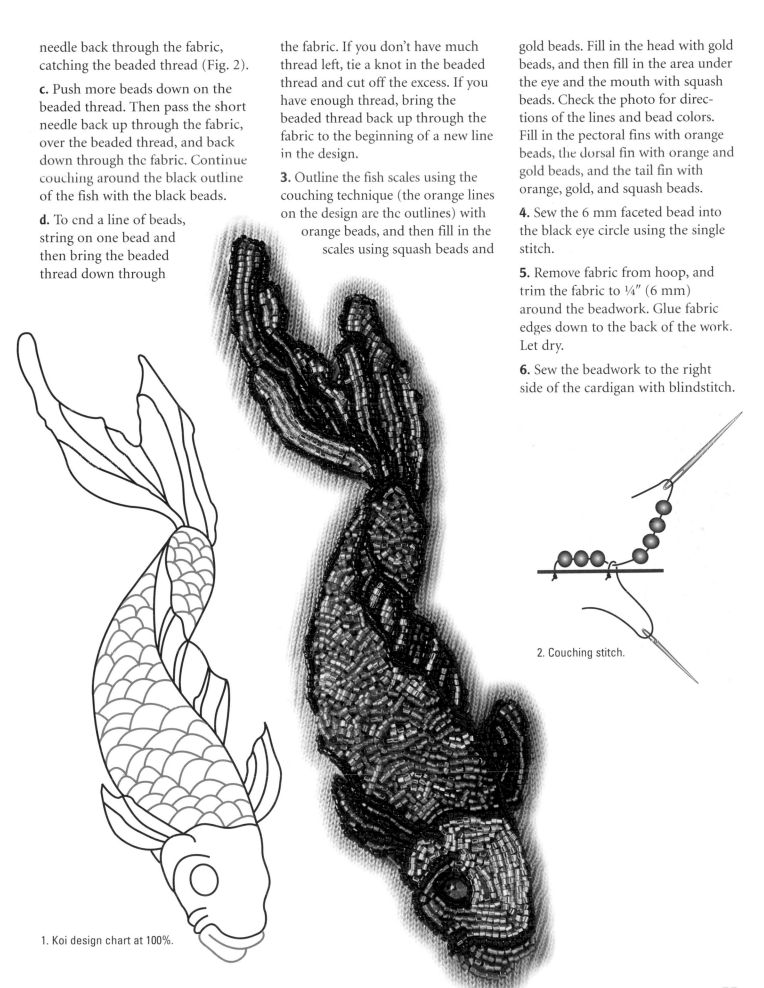

1. Koi design chart at 100%.

2. Couching stitch.

Daisy Chain Pants

Daisies shut their petals at night and open them with the sun. Their lovely round centers have an eyelike appearance. The word daisy comes from the Old English daeges eage, *which means "day's eye."*

Bellis perennis, *commonly known as the English daisy, is a small plant* with white, pink, or red petals. Since medieval times, this small daisy has been used to cure ills. The flowers and leaves are ground into a pulp and then the juice is extracted. This juice is used to heal bruises, sprains, and deep wounds. It has also been used to ease pain in the stomach and intes- tines, and to cure insanity. Daisies have been made into chains and used as adornment for centuries. Today we can even make daisy chains with beads, and what fun it is. Here is a project for all the daisy chain lovers out there.

MATERIALS *

6 mm glass pearl beads as follows:
- Light olive green, 24
- Navy blue, 24
- Maroon, 24

Maroon silver-lined size 8° charlotte beads, 10 g

Green/blue/maroon striped size 6° seed beads, 40 g

Beading needle, size 11

Black Nymo nylon monofilament beading thread, size F

Pair of long pants

Note: The number of beads will vary depending on the pants size. I used size 4.

1. Using 6 yd (5½ m) of thread, string on 10 striped beads.

a. Pass the needle back through the first bead strung on, forming a circle (the petal beads). Leave about a 6"

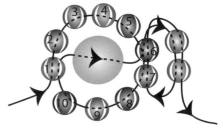

1. First daisy of the attached daisy chain stitch.

(15 cm) tail of thread to be tied off and woven in later.

b. String on 1 green pearl bead, and then pass the needle through the 6th striped bead strung on.

c. String on 2 striped beads (the attachment beads), and then pass the needle back through the 6th and 7th beads strung on. Then pass the needle back through the 2 attachment beads (Fig. 1).

d. String on 8 striped beads, and then pass the needle back through the 2nd bead of the attachment beads so the thread is coming out between the 2 attachment beads (Fig. 2).

e. String on 1 maroon pearl bead (Fig. 3). Pass the needle back through the 5th striped bead strung on the 8 petal beads.

f. String on 2 striped attachment beads. Pass the needle back through the 5th and 4th beads of the petal beads and then back through the attachment beads. Now there are two daisies.

g. Keep working in the daisy stitch. Alternate the 3 colors (green, maroon, and blue) for the center pearl beads. For every 4th daisy, use 12 maroon charlotte beads as the petal beads. Make 54 daisies or as many as it takes to fit around the pants waist. When finished, tie off and weave in the ends.

2. Sew the strand of daisies onto the waistband, using beading thread and the running stitch as follows:

a. Tie a knot in the end of the thread, and pass the needle up through the fabric close to the buttonhole. Then pass the needle through the first center pearl bead, back through the fabric, and out of the fabric, and then through the next center pearl bead.

Detail of pocket.

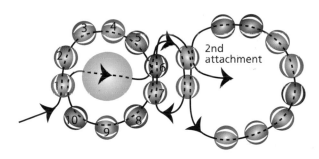

2. The petals of the 2nd daisy.

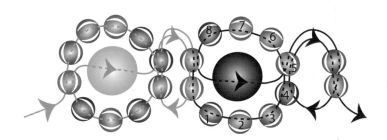

3. Attached daisy chain stitch.

b. Repeat along the waistband until the strand is sewn on. Tie off and hide the end of the thread through the beads. Cut off excess thread.

3. Make a 9-daisy strand of beads (or the number that will fit) for the pocket edge, starting and ending with a maroon-petaled daisy. Sew the daisies onto the pocket as you did for the waistband. Repeat for the other pocket.

Ari-Beaded Shorts

MATERIALS

Size 11° seed beads as follows:
- White matte, 5g
- Gold, 1
- Olive green-lined, 43

Green matte size 11° Japanese seed beads, 38

Green silver-lined matte size 11° Japanese seed beads, 32

White Delica beads, 5g

Green AB Delica beads, 32

Light blue transparent AB size 15° seed beads, 5 g

Black matte size 14° seed beads, 5 g

White AB transparent matte ½" twisted bugle beads, 7

Green AB transparent matte ½" twisted bugle beads, 11

Gold AB ¼" bugle beads, 35

DMC tatting thread, size 80, one small ball of each: olive green, black, and white

Crochet hook, size 10

Tambour needle handle

Tambour needle, size 70

Tambour hoop and stand

Tweezers

Tracing paper

Erasable fabric marker

Embroidery needle

Beige shorts or other garment to be decorated

Breeches, knickerbockers, knee pants, and shorts are all names given to pants with a hemline above, at or just below the knee. Breeches, knee-length pants with tight legs, were popular in the 18th century. These were worn with hose or stockings covering the lower leg. Knickerbockers and knee pants were primarily worn by boys in Europe and the United States in the late 1800s and early 1900s. Knickers were loose-fitting pants that had a buckled band at the knee, and knee pants were knee-length, tight-legged pants without a buckled band. These pants were usually worn with knee socks.

In the late 19th century, the British military, wanting to keep the troops posted in tropical regions cool and comfortable, issued the men short pants with wide legs. These soon became known as Bermuda shorts. After the turn of the 20th century, the Boy Scout uniform, which was modeled after Bermuda shorts, played a major role in making shorts popular. The shorts here are adorned with an egret fashioned with beads using the ari chain stitch. This pattern also would look wonderful on a blouse, dress, jacket, or skirt.

1. Trace the design (Fig. 1) onto the tracing paper using the erasable fabric marker. Place the left shorts leg into the tambour hoop right side up, and stretch it tight. Baste the tracing paper onto the shorts leg, making sure the design is straight. Put the tambour hoop into the stand. Tighten the tambour needle into the tambour handle with the

hook facing the screw on the handle, so it is easy to see where the hook is.

2. See Chapter 2 for details of how to ari-stitch. Start with the reeds, using the olive green tatting thread.

a. Place the ball of thread under the hoop, and hold the thread in your left hand (in your right hand if you are left-handed). With your right hand (left if you are left-handed), puncture the fabric at the bottom end of the first reed on the right side of the design.

b. With the hand under the hoop, secure a loop of thread onto the hook. Pull the needle out of the fabric, and pull the thread end through the fabric until there is about 8″ (20 cm) of thread.

c. Puncture the fabric again at a point adjacent to the 8″ (20 cm) thread end. Secure a loop of thread onto the hook, and pull the needle and the loop out of the fabric. Remove the needle from the loop, put the thread end through the loop, and pull tight. This anchors the thread to the fabric.

d. Puncture the fabric again at a point adjacent to the anchor thread, secure a loop of thread onto the hook, and pull the needle and the loop out of the fabric.

e. Take the needle out of the loop, and put a twisted green bugle bead onto the needle. Put the hook back on the loop. Slide the bead down the needle and onto the loop of thread, and push the bead down so it touches the fabric.

f. Keep the needle in the loop, and puncture the fabric at a point a little bit longer than the bead. Secure a loop of thread onto the hook, and pull the loop up through the fabric and through the loop with the bead on it. Pull the stitch tight by jerking the needle back and forth.

g. For the next 3 stitches, use green AB Delica beads. After these 4 beads, anchor the thread the same way as at the beginning of the line.

h. Skip the area where the bird's body is, and start the reed again on the other side of the bird's body. With a new thread and the ari chain stitch, finish the reed with 1 green bugle and 7 green AB Delica beads.

3. Follow the design chart and photo for bead color and placement, and ari chain stitch along the rest of the design lines, changing thread for each line: green thread for reeds, white thread for the bird's body, and black thread for the bird's legs, beak, and eye area. A new thread must be started every time lines start or stop. There will be many thread ends, and they will get in the way, so every so often they must be pulled through to the wrong side of the work (use the embroidery needle). Then make a knot for extra security, weave the thread ends into the stitches, and cut off the excess.

1. Egret design chart at 100%.

Closeup of beading of egret design, ari-beaded shorts.

Tambour-Beaded Moth Skirt

There are more than 100,000 different types of moth in the world, ranging from small to large and from plain to beautifully colored. Some fly at night and others during the day. Most moth antennae are feathered, although a few have clubbed antennae.

Amazingly enough, moths have ears. They use their ears mainly to detect the ultrasonic sound of bats, which are their primary predator, but also use them to hear other moths.

Moth ears are very thin membranes stretched over sensors. Some moths have their ears on their thoraxes, some on their abdomen, and others on their wings. Moths have always interested me, and when I saw a gorgeous one clinging to the wall of my porch, I had to honor it with this moth skirt. Done in the tambour stitch, it is a fun project. This design would be wonderful on the back of a thin jacket or dress as well as on a skirt.

MATERIALS

Matte size 8° seed beads as follows:
- Light blue, 10 g
- Beige, 7 g
- Blue, 5 g
- Lime green, 5 g
- Purple, 5 g

Blue flat disk beads (holes lengthwise through the bead), 7

Small light blue ball of DMC tatting thread, size 80 (or different colors to match the beads)

Twisted beading needle, size medium

Crochet hook, size 10

Tambour needle handle

Tambour needle, size 90

Tambour hoop and stand

Tracing paper

Erasable fabric marker

Wax-free tracing paper (fabric carbon paper)

Brown skirt or color of your choice

1. Enlarge and trace the moth design diagram (Fig. 1) using tracing paper and the marker, as follows:

a. Lay the skirt, inside out, on a hard surface. Place the carbon paper face down on the bottom edge of the wrong side of the skirt, and then place the traced design on top of the carbon paper.

b. Trace around the design, pressing hard. When you are finished, remove the tracing paper and the carbon paper. If the lines are too light or places were missed, go over the lines with the fabric marker.

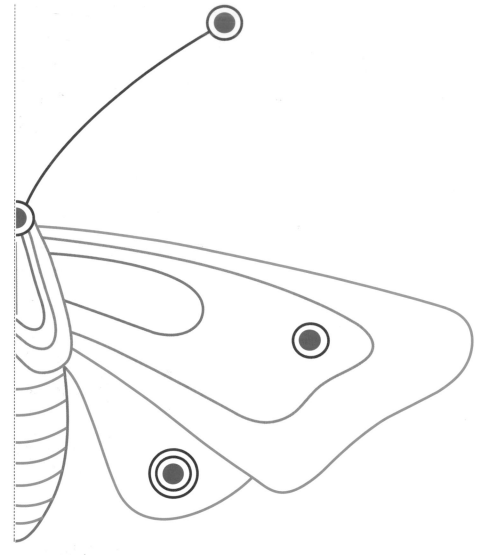

1. Half pattern for moth design chart at 100%. Trace on folded paper.

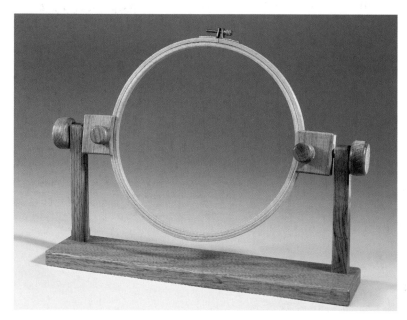

Tambour frame.

2. Place the skirt inside out in the tambour hoop, and stretch tight. Make sure the design is in the middle of the hoop, facing up. Then put the hoop in the stand.

3. Tighten the tambour needle into the tambour handle with the hook facing the screw on the handle, so it is easy to see where the hook is. Start with one antenna.

a. Using the twisted beading needle, string about 28 blue beads onto the tatting thread ball. (It's better to string on a few more beads than you think you will need because it is easier to take off extra beads when you are through than to run out of beads and have to add more to the ball of thread.) Keep the ball of beaded thread under the hoop.

b. Puncture the fabric with the tambour needle at the beginning of one of the antennae. Hold the tambour needle with the right hand, or with the left if you are left-handed. With the other hand under the hoop, secure a loop of thread onto the hook. Pull the needle out of the fabric, and pull the thread end through the fabric until there is about an 8″ (20 cm) length of thread. The hardest part of tambour stitch is getting the hook to come out of the fabric without catching on the fabric. But if the piece is kept stretched very tight in the hoop and if the pressure on the fabric as you pull the thread through is kept away from the hook, it doesn't seem to catch as much.

c. Puncture the fabric in a spot near the thread end, and secure a loop of thread onto the hook. Pull the hook and the loop through the fabric.

d. Remove the hook from the loop, put the thread end through the loop, and pull tight. This anchors the thread to the fabric.

Closeup of beading, moth skirt.

4. Slide a bead up the thread until it touches the fabric. Then:

a. Puncture the fabric with the needle at a point a little longer than 1 bead width from the anchor stitch.

b. Secure a loop of thread onto the hook, making sure the bead is between the fabric and the loop, and pull the loop through the fabric. Pull the stitch tight by jerking the needle back and forth.

c. With the needle in the loop, puncture the fabric, leaving a space a little longer than 1 bead width.

d. Slide a bead up to the fabric, secure a loop of thread onto the hook, and pull through the fabric. Tighten the stitch.

e. Keep stitching with the beads until you come to the end of the antennae. Make sure to tighten each stitch, and check the underside of the hoop every so often to make sure there are no loose stitches or twisted beads.

f. Anchor the thread by making a small stitch without a bead. Then pull the loop until it is about 8″ (20 cm) long, cut the thread loop at the top, and pull tight. With the hand under the hoop, pull the thread ball so the cut thread will come out of the fabric. Remove any excess beads from the thread ball.

5. Follow the design chart, and tambour-stitch along the rest of the design lines, stringing beads and changing thread for each line and color.

6. When all the design is beaded, turn the hoop around in the stand so the beads are on top, and seed-stitch the disk beads in the middle of each of the circles on the antennae, the wings, and the head.

7. After all the disk beads have been sewn on, tie off every thread end with a small knot for extra security. Weave all the thread ends into the chains using the crochet hook. Cut off the excess thread ends.

Bead-Embroidered Formal Dress

The father of French haute couture was Charles Fredrick Worth, an Englishman born in Bourne, Lincolnshire, in 1825. Before Charles Worth, a woman would tell her dressmaker how she wanted a dress designed. Worth designed his own dresses and had samples made to show clients.

After Napoleon III's wife, Empress Eugenie, saw a dress that Worth had designed and became a client, his success was ensured. He became the dressmaker for royalty. As the arbiter of fashion, one of his major changes was to do away with the crinoline or full underskirt, which had lasted for decades, and replace it with the bustle. Adding some beautiful bead embroidery to your dress will put you in the height of fashion.

MATERIALS

Size 11° seed beads as follows:
- Pale jade green, 7 g
- Pearly cream, 7 g
- Amber silver-lined, 7 g

Shiny white Delica beads, 7 g

Purple-lined Delica beads, 7 g

Off-white matte size 14° seed beads, 7 g

White Nymo nylon monofilament beading thread, size D

Beading needle, size 12

Erasable fabric marker

Tracing paper

Tweezers

Formal dress

Note: You may have to adjust the placement of the design and scattered beads to fit the neckline of your dress.

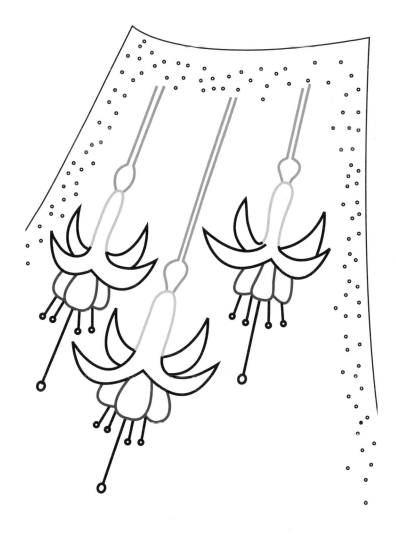

1. Fuchsia design chart for dress at 100%.

Closeup of beading.

1. Trace the design (Fig. 1) onto the tracing paper with the fabric marker. Place the design on one side of the dress, on the right side of the fabric, and baste the paper onto the dress with beading thread.

2. Using about 2 yd (183 cm) of thread, backstitch the beads onto the dress. If your dress has a lining, make sure to keep the thread in between the lining and the outer fabric so the thread will be hidden. Start by backstitching the stems (Fig. 2). Then outline the flowers with backstitch. Backstitch around

and around inside the outline until the flower is filled in with beads. Follow the bead colors in Figure 1 and in the closeup photo. Repeat for the other two flowers.

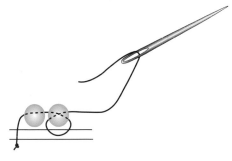

2. Backstitch.

3. Seed-stitch the neckline beads, scattering them randomly around the neckline. Use the six bead colors from the flowers.

4. Remove the basting thread and the tracing paper from around and under the beads. Use the tweezers on hard-to-reach pieces of paper.

5. Repeat Steps 1 through 4 for the other side of the dress, but first take the traced design and flip the tracing paper over so the design mirrors the first side of the dress.

Lotus Flower Bathing Suit

The lotus flower held great meaning for the ancient Egyptians, symbolizing among other things creation and the sun. In one of the Egyptian creation stories, the sun god Ra created himself from the primordial sea, called Nun, emerging on a mound of earth from the opening petals of a lotus flower.

What better way to soak up the sun's rays than by sporting a beaded lotus flower on your bathing suit? The flower is made using the lane stitch and the stacked seed stitch. The edging on the suit is done in beaded needle tatting. The flower could easily decorate the back of a jacket as well.

MATERIALS

Size 11° seed beads as follows:
- Off-white pearl, 5 g
- Pink transparent, 15 g
- Pink-lined, 5 g
- Red transparent matte, 5 g
- Red silver-lined AB, 5 g
- Yellow opaque, 5 g

Off-white cotton crochet thread, size 10

White Nymo nylon monofilament beading thread, size D

Tatting needle, size 7

Twisted beading needle, size medium

Beading needle, size 11

Embroidery needle (to punch holes in tracing paper around design)

Erasable fabric marker

Pounce and pounce powder

Tracing paper

Two-piece bathing suit

Suit Top

1. To make the tatted edging on one side of the bathing suit top, string 260 pink transparent beads onto the crochet thread ball, using the twisted beading needle. Remove the beading needle, and thread on the tatting needle. Skip about 2 yd (183 cm) of thread, and begin tatting at that point. The beads in this piece are worked into all the picots. (See the beaded needle tatting section of Chapter 2 for how to tat with beads.)

a. To make the first ring (Fig. 1), follow this pattern: 3 double stitches, a 5-bead picot, 3 double stitches, a 5-bead picot, 3 double stitches, a 4-bead picot, and 3 double stitches. Then close the ring (cl), and reverse work (rw).

3. Second bead-tatted ring has been added.

Closeup of tatted edge.

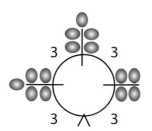

1. First bead-tatted ring.

b. To make the chain (Fig. 2) attached to the ring, follow this pattern: *3 double stitches, 5-bead picot, 3 double stitches, 5-bead picot, 3 double stitches; then cl and rw (close the ring and reverse the work).

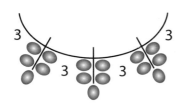

2. Bead-tatted chain.

c. The second ring (Fig. 3) follows this pattern: *3 double stitches, join (J) to the 4-bead picot from the first ring, 3 double stitches, 5-bead picot, 3 double stitches, 4-bead picot, 3 double stitches; then close the ring and reverse the work. Make the second chain the same as the first.*

d. Repeat between the asterisks until there are 10 rings and 10 chains, or enough to cover one side of the bathing suit top.

e. Make the 11th ring following this pattern: 3 double stitches, J (join),

3 double stitches, 5-bead picot, 3 double stitches, 5-bead picot, 3 double stitches; then close the ring.

f. Cut the thread, leaving about 6″ (15 cm) of thread. Tie a knot to secure the tatting so it won't unravel, and then use the tatting needle to hide the thread end in several stitches. Cut off the excess thread. Use the running stitch and white beading thread to sew the tatting to the bathing suit top.

2. Repeat Step 1 for the other side of the bathing suit top.

4. Lotus flower design chart at 100%.

Closeup of lotus flower.

Suit Bottom

3. Repeat the tatting pattern for the edging on the bathing suit bottom, using 615 beads. There will be 26 rings and 25 chains. This amount might have to be adjusted depending on the size of the bathing suit used.

4. To make the lotus flower on the bathing suit bottom, trace the design onto the tracing paper (Fig. 4). Transfer the design to the bathing suit using the pounce transfer method (see Chapter 1), or use the transfer method of your choice.

a. Using the lane stitch and white beading thread, bead-embroider the petals of the flower. (For an example of bead colors and placement on a petal, see Fig. 5.) Start with an inside petal. All the petals have off-white pearl size 11° seed

beads on their tips, with pink-lined beads next, then pink transparent, then red transparent, and finally red silver-lined AB. Work around the inside petals, and then move on to the outside petals.

5. Petal design chart (enlarged). Adapt shape and number of beads to outline.

b. When all the petals are done, make the center of the flower using the yellow beads and the stacked seed stitch (Fig. 6). Randomly vary the length of each stacked stitch from 2 to 5 beads long.

6. Stacked seed stitch.

4

Accessories

Bead-Embroidered Necklace

Who would have thought that an irritant could turn into something as beautiful as a pearl? Pearls can be found in oysters, mussels, clams, scallops, and even in conches and abalone. Pearls come in many shapes, sizes, and colors.

Before the early 20th century and the invention of cultured pearls, the rarity of pearls made them accessible only to the nobility or the very rich. Pearls are readily available today because of several enterprising Japanese who discovered that if a nucleus, generally

a small piece of mussel shell, is inserted into the mantle of a mollusk, the animal will create a pearl on demand, a cultured pearl. The addition of pearls to this bead-embroidered necklace enhances its beauty.

MATERIALS

Accent beads of your choice, 7
Pill-shaped pearl beads, 17
Maroon niblet beads, 21
Light blue disk beads, 10
Red ultrasuede, ¼ yd (23 cm)
White or natural color
 linen, ¼ yd (23 cm)
Delica beads, as follows:
 • Silver-lined gold, 7 g
 • Silver-lined red, 7 g
 • Opaque turquoise, 4 g
 • Silver-lined turquoise satin, 4 g
 • Silver-lined mint green satin, 4 g
 • Light green matte, 4 g
Green AB (iridescent) 1/4" (6 mm)
 bugle beads, 7 g

Size 11° seed beads as follows:
 • Dark green, 4 g
 • Blue lined, 5 g
 • Opaque mint green, 5 g
White size 8° charlotte beads, 145
Light blue AB size 15° two-cuts, 2 g
Beading needle, size 11
Sewing needle
White Nymo nylon monofilament
 beading thread, size D
Erasable fabric marker
Tracing paper
Embroidery hoop
Embroidery scissors
Sewing scissors

Note: You may have to adjust the colors and kinds of beads used, depending on the accent beads chosen.

1. Use the template transfer method (see Chapter 1) and the erasable fabric marker to transfer the necklace diagram (Fig. 1) onto the linen. Then place the linen into the embroidery hoop, keeping the fabric tight and the design in the middle of the hoop.

2. Proceed as follows, using the photo and diagram for guidance.

a. Sew 6 of the accent beads in place using the seed stitch.

b. Seed-stitch the pearls, maroon niblets, and light blue disks in place. Let the beads chosen as accent beads dictate the exact placement.

c. Sew the bugle beads in place along the edges of the necklace (see photo).

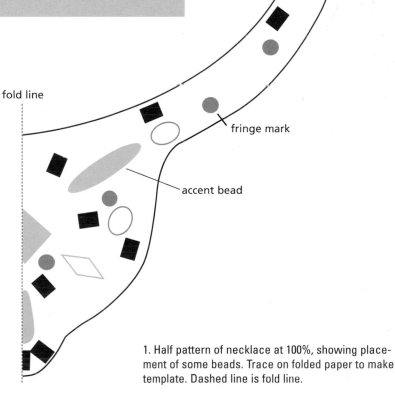

light blue disk bead

pearl

niblets

fold line

fringe mark

accent bead

1. Half pattern of necklace at 100%, showing placement of some beads. Trace on folded paper to make template. Dashed line is fold line.

d. Backstitch down the rest of the beads (Fig. 2), filling in the entire necklace surface (see the photo for bead color and placement).

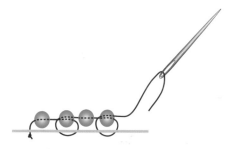

2. Backstitch.

3. Remove the linen from the hoop, and:

a. Cut out the fabric with the beads, leaving a ½″ (1 cm) seam allowance all around the outline.

b. Use the template to cut out a backing from the ultrasuede the same size as the cut-out beaded linen.

c. Pin the ultrasuede, right side out, to the back of the beaded linen, folding under the linen and ultra-suede seam allowances. Sew ultra-suede and linen together, using the blind stitch.

4. Zipper-stitch (see Chapter 2) an edging all around the necklace, except where the fringe is, as follows:

a. Make a knot in the end of about 2 yd (183 cm) of beading thread, and pass the needle through the outside edge of the necklace at a point where one of the fringe marks is (Fig. 1), making sure the knot is hidden in the seam. Then:

b. String on 1 gold, 1 red, and 1 gold Delica bead.

c. Make a small stitch in the fabric about ⅛″ (3 mm) from the place where the thread is coming out of the fabric. Then pass the needle back through the last gold bead strung on.

d. *String on 1 red and 1 gold Delica bead, make a small stitch in the fabric, and pass the needle back through the last bead strung on.*

e. Repeat between the asterisks all around the necklace edges, until you get to where the other fringe mark is (see Figure 1).

5. Using the basic fringe method (see Chapter 2), make the fringe in increasing lengths from the smallest at the edge to the longest in the middle, using beads to match the colors of the necklace (see photo for guidance).

a. Increase the size of the fringe every 6 fringes.

b. Use the 7th accent bead for the end of the middle fringe (center front).

c. When you are making the fringe under the bugle beads, pass the thread through the bugle beads instead of the fabric to make a fringe that appears to include the bugles.

6. Make one side of the clasp at the back of the neck by threading a beading needle onto 1 yd (1 m) of beading thread. Make a knot on the end, and pass the needle through the fabric at the tip of one end of the necklace. Then:

a. String on 2 red Delica beads, 1 pearl, 2 red Delica beads, 2 gold Delica beads, 1 pearl, and 1 red Delica bead.

b. Pass the needle back through the last pearl bead strung on, the 2 gold Delica beads, the 2 red Delica beads, and the first pearl.

c. String on 2 red Delica beads, and pass the needle through the fabric at the end of the necklace next to where the first 2 red Delica beads are.

d. Pass the needle back through all the beads several times to secure them, and then make a knot hidden in the seam. Cut off the excess.

e. Repeat on the other end of the necklace, only instead of the last pearl bead, string on a ring of Delica beads big enough to fit over the last pearl on the other end of the necklace (see lower photo).

Details of necklace.

Pink Hibiscus Visor

Hibiscus is native to Asia and the Pacific Islands and is the state flower of Hawaii and the national flower of Malaysia. In the ancient past, the hibiscus was used as makeup to darken women's eyebrows. It also has medicinal qualities and is and was used to cure fever, headaches, and skin troubles. Hibiscus is used in many herbal teas. The loomed, stylized hibiscus on this visor is sure to please. It could be used for a matching belt as well.

MATERIALS

Delica beads as follows:
- Yellow opaque AB (iridescent), 5 g
- Green bean opaque matte, 5 g
- Dark purple opaque, 5 g
- Olive green AB, 5 g
- Dark red matte, 5 g
- Rose opaque, 7 g
- Sapphire silver-lined, 7 g
- Metallic teal iris, 10 g

Black Nymo nylon monofilament beading thread, size F
Beading needle, size 11
Beading loom
Bonding glue
Scissors
Denim visor

1. See Chapter 2 for instructions on how to do loom bead weaving. Warp the loom with 10 warp threads, each 3′ (1 m) long, using the black thread. Then:

a. Attach the weft thread to the left outermost warp thread, leaving a tail 2′ (61 cm) long for making the thread cloth later on.

b. Use the size 11 beading needle to weave the beads, following the design chart (Fig. 1), reading it from left to right, and from bottom to top. Repeat the design 18 times or however many times you need to fill the space on your visor. Remember to make the first and last row using all sapphire beads. The finished loomwork should measure ½″ (1 cm) wide and long enough to fit around your visor.

c. End by weaving ⅜″ (10 mm) of thread cloth to hold the beads tightly onto the warp threads. (See Loom Bead Weaving section on how to make thread cloth.) Next make a ⅜″ (10 mm) thread cloth on the other side of the work.

d. Remove the beaded piece from the loom, and tie off all pairs of warp thread with square knots. Cut off the excess thread, and fold the thread cloth to the back of the work. If necessary, glue in place.

2. Put glue on the visor, and press the beaded work in place. Let dry.

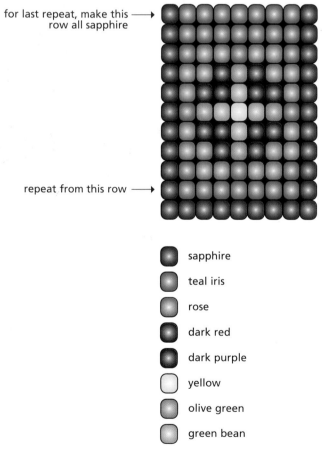

for last repeat, make this → row all sapphire

repeat from this row →

- sapphire
- teal iris
- rose
- dark red
- dark purple
- yellow
- olive green
- green bean

1. Hibiscus design chart.

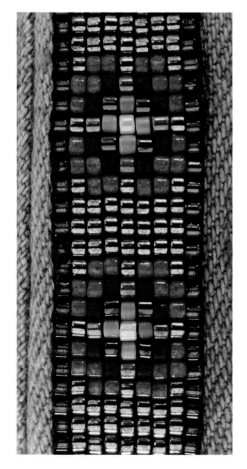

Closeup of visor beading.

Norwegian Beret

This lovely design was inspired by the traditional folk costumes or bunads of Norway, which are worn for weddings, holidays, and festive occasions. They were originally rural peasant costumes, but in the early 1900s people all over Norway wanted to preserve the "old ways," and bunads became increasingly popular. Designs on the old folk costumes varied more than they do today, because women used to personalize their own bunads. Bodice insets, belts, and caps are the parts most frequently bead-embroidered. Some bunads from the Hordaland Region in Norway feature bugle and seed beads in distinctive snowflake-like patterns. When I first saw one of these bunads, I fell in love with the design. This project looks impressive, yet it is easy to make.

MATERIALS

½" (12 mm) bugle beads as follows:
- White matte twisted, 4
- Blue iris matte, 28
- Yellow iris matte, 28
- Green matte twisted, 28
- Dark pink matte, 4

¾" (2 cm) bugle beads as follows:
- White opaque, 40
- Dark pink AB twisted, 36

Size 11° seed beads as follows:
- White opaque, 5 g
- Silver-lined lavender, 5 g
- Pink transparent, 5 g
- Green transparent, 5 g
- Light yellow opaque, 5 g

White Nymo nylon monofilament
  beading thread, size D
Beading needle, size 11
Embroidery scissors
Erasable fabric marker
Gray woolen beret

The basic concept is to make an X of beads and then fill it in with other beads.

1. Find the center of the beret, and mark with the marker. Knot the end of a 2 yd (183 cm) length of thread, and bring the needle up through the center mark. Then:

a. Using seed stitch bead embroidery (see Chapter 2), sew 1 green seed bead in the center of the beret. Bring the thread back out to the right side of the beret, right next to the green seed bead.

b. String on 1 lavender bead, 1 pink twisted bugle bead, and 1 lavender bead. Push the needle through the fabric at a point where the beads will lie next to the green center bead and at a distance a little bit longer than the 3 beads, so they will lie flat. Go on to make an X shape with 3 more lavender-pink-lavender lines of beads. The rest of the design works

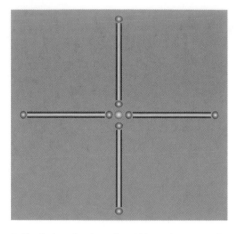

1. Bugle beads placed at 90° angles to each other.

off this shape, so it is important to make sure the bead lines are placed at 90° angles to each other (Fig. 1).

2. Now you will use the satin stitch. Bring the needle up next to the edge closest to the center of the beret of one of the pink twisted bugle beads. Then:

a. *String on 1 light yellow seed bead, 1 white ¾" bugle bead, and 1 light yellow seed bead. Sew these beads on so they lie parallel to the pink twisted bugle bead. Then bring the needle up next to the edge of the white bugle bead that is closest to the center of the beret.* Repeat between the asterisks four times.

b. String on 1 lavender seed bead, 1 pink twisted bugle bead, and 1 lavender seed bead. Sew these beads down in the same manner as the white bugle beads. Repeat until you have 4 pink twisted bugle bead lines.

c. String on 1 green seed bead, 1 blue ½" bugle bead, and 1 green seed bead. Sew these beads on so they are parallel to the pink twisted bugle beads. Repeat two times.

3. Repeat Step 2 on all sides of the pink twisted bugle beads that form the X shape.

4. Fill in the holes in between the bugle bead lines with pink seed

beads, using the seed stitch bead embroidery technique.

5. Start a new thread if you have used up the 2 yd (183 cm) of thread, and bring the needle up to the right side of the beret at the center point of one of the Vs made by the white, pink, and blue bugle beads of the main body of the snowflake. The needle should be coming out even with the side of the white bugle bead nearest to one of the pink bugle beads that form the X. Then:

a. String on 1 pink seed bead, 1 green twisted bugle bead, and 1 pink seed bead. Sew these beads down so the line they make is parallel to the ends of the light yellow seed beads on the ends of the white bugle beads that are already laid down.

b. Repeat Step a two more times.

c. String on 1 white seed bead, 1 yellow bugle bead, and 1 white seed bead. Sew these down parallel to the green bugle beads you added in Steps a and b, and repeat two more times.

6. Repeat Step 5 seven times.

7. Fill in the holes in between the bugle bead lines with light yellow seed beads, using the same seed stitch bead-embroidery technique as in Step 4. The main snowflake is now done (Fig. 2).

8. Make the four flower snowflakes. These are placed above each of the Vs made by the blue bugle beads, as follows:

a. Start a new thread, and bring the needle out about 1¼" (3 cm) away from the center point of one of the blue Vs. String on 1 green seed bead for the center, and sew it down.

b. Bring the needle up next to the green bead, and single-bead back-stitch 7 white seed beads all around the green bead, forming a small flower (Fig. 3).

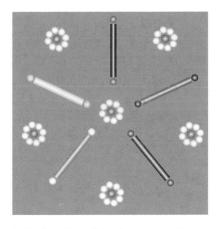

3. Design chart of the flower snowflakes.

2. Design chart of the main snowflake.

c. Bring the needle out about ⅛″ (3 mm) away from the small flower at a point at the top of the flower straight up from the center point of the blue V.

d. String on 1 white seed bead, 1 yellow ½″ bugle bead, and 1 white seed bead. Sew down.

e. See Fig. 3 for position of the 5 bugle bead lines that radiate out from the small flower. Each bugle bead line that radiates out from the flower is a different color. The other four bugle bead lines are the following color combinations:

- 1 lavender seed bead, 1 pink ½″ bugle bead, and 1 lavender seed bead;

- 1 green seed bead, 1 blue bugle bead, and 1 green seed bead;

- 1 yellow seed bead, 1 white ½″ twisted bugle bead, and 1 yellow seed bead;

- 1 pink seed bead, 1 green twisted bugle bead, and 1 pink seed bead.

f. After sewing these lines down, make the five small flowers that are placed in between each pair of bugle bead lines in the same way you made the small center flower in Step 8b. Use green seed beads for the centers of the flowers and white seed beads for the petals.

g. The other four flower snowflakes are made in the same way, but the centers of the white flowers are made with different colored seed beads. One snowflake flower should have light yellow seed bead centers, one snowflake flower should have lavender seed bead centers, and the last snowflake flower should have pink seed bead centers. See photo for reference.

Daisy Chain Hatband

The finest and most famous of all straw hats is the Panama hat. The people of South America have been wearing straw hats to protect themselves from the sun since 4000 BC. Ancient straw hats were more like scarves. In the early 1500s, the Spanish conquistadors found the indigenous people wearing straw hats made of a wonderful translucent straw weave. In the early 1600s, the Spanish used Ecuadorian weavers to make hats in a European style. By the 1800s, these hats had made their way to Europe and North America by way of Panama, a trade center, thus the name Panama hat. The straw hat shown in this project has a beautiful daisy chain hatband.

MATERIALS *

Silver-lined lavender matte size 6°
seed beads, 31
Purple-lined size 6° seed beads, 31
Gold size 11° seed beads, 7 g
Size 8° seed beads as follows:
- Orange transparent matte, 31
- Pale yellow transparent matte, 31
- Lime green transparent matte, 60
- Raspberry red transparent matte, 32
- Root beer transparent matte, 30
- Amber transparent matte, 33
- Red-orange transparent matte, 31

Black Nymo nylon monofilament
beading thread, size D
Beading needle, size 12
Straw hat with a wide, floppy brim

*Note: Numbers of beads are
estimates. They will vary depending on
the distance around the hat.*

1. Use about 4 yd (366 cm) of thread. Then:

a. String on 1 orange size 8°, 1 gold size 11°, 1 lime green size 8°, 1 gold size 11°, 1 amber size 8°, 1 gold size 11°, 1 raspberry red size 8°, and 1 gold size 11° bead. Pass the needle back through the first (orange) bead, forming a circle.

b. String on 1 lavender size 6° bead, pass the needle back through the pale yellow bead, and pull tight. This forms the first daisy (Fig. 1).

1. Daisy chain stitch.

c. String on 3 gold size 11° beads, forming the stem.

2. Keep working using the daisy chain stitch and the three gold stem beads until you have 62 daisies or until your daisy chain will go around the crown of the hat with about 7 daisies left on each end to dangle down the brim. Every daisy should have 4 gold size 11° beads and 1 lime green size 8° bead, but the other colors should be random, using the other size 8° bead colors. For the daisy centers, alternate purple and lavender size 6 beads.

3. When you are finished, make two small knots in between the closest beads to the end, and then weave the thread end through the end daisies until they are secure. Cut off the excess.

4. Thread the needle on about 2 yd (183 cm) of thread, and knot the end. Then:

a. Sew the daisy chain onto the base of the crown of the hat, using the running stitch. Start sewing down at the 8th daisy from the end of the chain, and place it in the middle of one of the sides of the hat. I put mine on the right side. When you are sewing the band onto the hat, pass the needle through the purple and lavender size 6° seed beads.

b. If your hat has a sweatband, hide the thread under it. When you are finished, tie an overhand knot in the daisy chain, and let the chain ends dangle down the brim (Fig. 2).

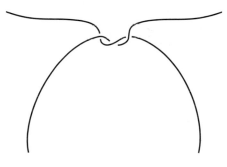

2. Overhand knot for the beaded daisy chain.

Daisy Headband

Headbands have been around for centuries. The ancient Egyptians wore ornate gold-and-gemstone diadems, and Sumerian women in Mesopotamia wore leather headbands. Kings and queens in ancient Greece and Rome wore bands of cloth, often embellished with jewels, tied around their heads to signify their royal status. Crowns, tiaras, and wreaths evolved from these ancient headbands. The headband in this project is done with a variety of stitches including backstitch, seed stitch, detached chain stitch, and daisy edging. Use your imagination for more fun by experimenting with different colors.

MATERIALS

White Delica beads, 10 g
Opaque yellow Delica beads, 5 g
Translucent green charlotte beads, 5 g
White Nymo nylon monofilament beading thread, Size D
Beading needle, size 11 or 12
Fabric headband about 2″ (5 cm) wide with a Velcro closure*

Note: The headband we used has two layers of fabric.

1. To make the edging, tie a knot at the end of about 3 yd (274 cm) of thread. Pass the needle through the fabric at the edge of one end of the headband, making sure that the knot is hidden in the seam.

2. String on 1 white Delica bead, 1 yellow Delica bead, 1 white Delica bead, 1 green charlotte bead, and 1 white Delica bead. Push the beads down the thread until they touch the fabric. Then pass the needle back through the yellow bead, going through the bead in the opposite direction (Fig. 1).

3. String on 1 more white Delica bead, and pass the needle through the fabric of the edge of the headband about ⅛″ (3 mm) away from the beads. Bring the needle out of the fabric about ⅛″ (3 mm) from where it went in. Pull tight (Fig. 1).

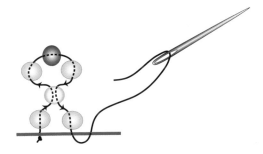

1. Daisy edge stitch.

4. Repeat the daisy edge stitch described above all along one edge of the headband. If you run out of thread, make a double overhand knot, and hide it in the seam. Then start a new thread.

5. Repeat Steps 1 through 4 on the other edge of the headband.

6. Transfer the daisy pattern (Fig. 2) onto the headband fabric, using your favorite transfer technique, centering the design on the length of the headband.

7. Use about 6 yd (549 cm) of thread so you don't run out. Knot the end of the thread, and pass the needle through the seam between the layers of fabric to hide the knot. Then bring the needle out to the right side of the fabric through one of the end daisy designs drawn on the headband.

8. To make the daisy petals of the small daisies on the ends, use the detached chain stitch (Fig. 3; also see Chapter 2). Each petal of the small daisies uses 7 white Delica beads. After making the petals, randomly sew on 8 or 9 yellow Delica beads to form the center, using the seed stitch (see Chapter 2 for seed stitch).

9. Make the stems using 3-bead backstitch units (Fig. 4; also see Chapter 2). Use the detached chain stitch and 11 green charlotte beads to make each leaf.

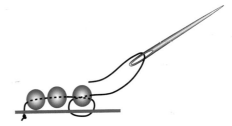

4. Three-bead backstitch.

10. For each large daisy, use the detached chain stitch and 17 white Delica beads for each petal. Use the seed stitch and 12 yellow Delica beads to fill the center.

11. Make the stem between the next two daisies as in Step 9.

12. The middle daisy is a little larger than the two small daisies on the ends. Use 9 white Delica beads for each petal and 10 yellow Delica beads for the center.

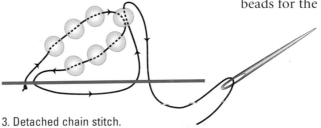

3. Detached chain stitch.

2. Daisy design chart at 100%.

Bone Bead Tatted Headband

Some of the earliest beads were fashioned from bones. Native Americans made tubular beads from shells, bone, copper, and stone that were anywhere from 1½" (4 cm) to 6" (15 cm) in length. When the Europeans came to North America, they noticed that these long beads were being used as hair ornamentation and thus called them hair-pipes. The Europeans began hand-drilling shell hair-pipes for use in trade with the Native Americans. In the mid to late 1800s, shell was replaced with bone, which was cheaper and didn't break as easily. Soon the Native Americans were making elaborate breastplates with bone hair-pipes, for use in various ceremonies and dances and as symbols of prosperity. This bone bead tatted headband will look great in your hair.

MATERIALS

Bone 6 mm round beads, 40
Bone 3 mm round beads, 42
Bone-colored size 6º triangle beads, 264
Tatting needle, size 5
Natural color cotton crochet thread, size 10
Twisted beading needle, size medium
Embroidery needle
White Nymo nylon monofilament beading thread, size D
Embroidery scissors
⅜" (10 mm) off-white elastic, 8" (20 cm)

The headband is made up of 2 rows of rings and chains, connected by picots. See the general tatting instructions in Chapter 2 for tatting basics.

1. Use the twisted beading needle to string the beads onto the crochet thread ball:

a. String on the beads in this order: *6 triangle beads, 2 small round bone beads, 1 large round bone bead, 6 triangle beads, 2 small round bone beads, and 1 large round bone bead.*

b. Repeat between the asterisks 19 times until you have added on 20 large round bone beads, and then string on 6 triangle beads, 2 small round bone beads, and 6 triangle beads.

c. Remove the twisted beading needle, and thread on the size 5 tatting needle. Start tatting about 1½ yd (137 cm) from the needle.

Row 1

a. To make the first ring (Fig. 1), follow this pattern: 3 double stitches, 6-bead picot with triangle beads, 3 double stitches, 2-bead picot with small bone beads, 3 double stitches, 6-bead picot with triangle beads, 3 double stitches; then close the ring (cl), and reverse the work (rw).

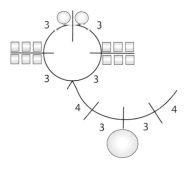

1. First bead-tatted ring.

b. To make the chain, follow this pattern: *4 double stitches, 1 picot (no beads), 3 double stitches, 1-bead picot with large bone bead, 3 double

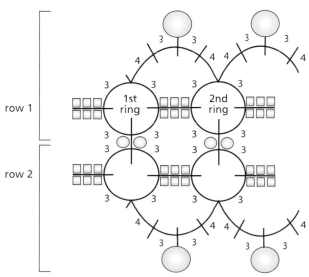

2. Bead-tatted chain is attached to the first ring.

stitches, 1 picot (no beads), 4 double stitches; then close the ring and reverse the work (Fig. 2).

c. The second ring follows this pattern (see Fig. 3): 3 double stitches, join (J) to the 2nd 6-bead picot on the previous ring, 3 double stitches, 2-bead picot with small bone beads, 3 double stitches, 6-bead picot with triangle beads, 3 double stitches; then close the ring and reverse the work.*

d. Repeat between the asterisks (steps b and c) 19 times. Tie a square knot, and hide the excess thread through several stitches. Cut off the thread end.

Row 2

a. Thread the twisted beading needle onto the crochet thread ball. String on *6 triangle beads and 1 large bone bead.* Repeat between the asterisks 19 times, and then string on 12 triangle beads.

b. Remove the twisted beading needle, and thread on the size 5 tatting needle. Start tatting about 1½ yd (137 cm) from the needle. (The rows will be attached with the rings facing each other and the chains facing out.)

c. To make the first ring, follow this pattern: 3 double stitches, 6-bead picot with triangle beads, 3 double stitches, join (J) to the 2-bead picot from row 1, 3 double stitches, 6-bead picot with triangle beads, 3 double stitches; then close the ring and reverse the work.

d. *Make the chain the same as in row 1 (see Fig. 2). Make the second ring following this pattern: 3 double stitches, J (join) to the 2nd 6-bead picot from the previous ring, 3 double stitches, J (join) to the corresponding 2-bead picot from row 1, 3 double stitches, 6-bead picot with triangle beads, 3 double stitches; close the ring and reverse the work* (see Fig. 3).

e. Repeat between the asterisks 19 times. Tie a square knot, and hide the excess thread through several stitches. Cut off the thread end.

To Finish

Make a small hem on both ends of the elastic, and sew it to both ends of the tatted piece. Adjust the elastic length so the headband fits snugly around your head.

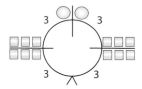

3. Start of the first and second rows.

Fringed Hair Elastics

MATERIALS

Pendant-style leaf beads of various
   greens, 8
Pink flower beads, 3
Yellow size 11° seed beads, 3
Olive green Delica beads, 80
Beading needle, size 11
Black Nymo nylon monofilament
   beading thread, size D
Hair elastic

■ Thread the needle onto about 2 yd (183 cm) of thread, and make a knot on the end. Pass the needle through the hair elastic from the inside to the outside of the band. This design has three fringes:

First Fringe

a. String on 3 olive green beads and 1 leaf bead (Fig. 1). Pass the needle back through the last 2 olive green beads strung on.

b. String on 6 olive green beads. String on 1 olive green bead and 1 leaf, and pass the needle back through the 1 olive green bead (Fig. 2).

c. String on 9 olive green beads and 1 leaf bead (Fig. 2). Pass the needle back through the last 3 olive green beads.

2. First fringe: Pass the needle back through the olive-colored beads that are in a straight line.

1. Start of the first branched fringe.

Rubber is made from the milky white sap called latex, which oozes out of the rubber tree. The natives of South America have been using rubber for over 600 years. In the 1800s, several technological advances in Europe made rubber use widespread there. After the American Charles Goodyear invented vulcanized rubber, which stood up to hot and cold much better than the rubber of the day, rubber products proliferated. In 1845, Stephen Perry of London patented the rubber band, which he had invented as a way to hold papers together. The flower hair elastic described in the directions uses the branched fringe technique. The other photos show other fringe techniques.

d. String on 8 olive green beads, 1 flower, and 1 yellow bead. Pass the needle back through the flower bead and then through the olive beads on the main row, but not the ones that branch out with the leaf beads. Pass the needle through the hair elastic and then back through the hair elastic so the needle comes out right next to the fringe you just made (Fig. 2).

Second Fringe

a. String on 6 olive green beads and 1 leaf. Pass the needle back through the last 2 olive green beads.

b. String on 6 olive green beads and 1 leaf, and pass the needle back through the last 3 olive green beads.

c. String on 9 olive green beads and 1 leaf, and pass the needle back through the last 4 olive green beads.

d. String on 3 olive green beads, 1 flower, and 1 yellow bead. Pass the needle back through the flower bead and then straight through 15 olive green beads until you get to the hair elastic.

e. Pass the needle first through the elastic and then back through the elastic so the needle comes out next to the first fringe made.

Third Fringe

a. String on 5 olive green beads and 1 leaf, and then pass the needle back through the last 3 olive green beads strung on.

b. String on 6 olive green beads and 1 leaf, and then pass the needle back through the last 2 olive green beads strung on.

c. String on 7 olive green beads, 1 flower, and 1 yellow bead. Pass the needle back through the flower bead and the 13 olive green beads until you get to the elastic. Pass the needle through the elastic, make a knot, and hide the thread end in the band. Cut off the excess.

See the photos for other hair elastic fringe ideas.

Some other fringe styles.

Knitted Scarf with Twisted Fringe

Knitting has been around for so long that no one knows its exact origins. The earliest piece of true knitting that we have is a pair of liturgical gloves excavated in Egypt. These were worn by bishops from the years 600 to 800 AD. Three fragments of fabric that appear to have been knitted from before 256 AD (made with either Eastern cross-stitch knitting or nal-binding) were found in an excavation on the site of the ancient city of Dura-Europos in Syria. Nalbinding (single-needle knitting) is an ancient form of knitting done with a large sewing needle and a short length of yarn. Series of yarn loops are made with the needle and the knitter's thumb. When the short length of yarn is almost used up, another length of yarn must be spliced onto the end. The scarf shown here is hand-knitted and is accented with twisted fringe.

MATERIALS

Amethyst chip stone beads, 128
Aqua and peridot size 4 mm faceted Czech fire-polished beads, 46
Blue iris size 8° charlotte beads, 10 g
Size 11° Japanese seed beads as follows:
  • Jade, 7 g
  • Emerald AB, 7 g
  • Lavender-lined transparent, 7 g
  • Purple transparent AB, 7 g
Light blue transparent AB two-cut size 15° seed beads, 7 g
Silver arrow-shaped charms, 10
Blue iris flower beads, 12
Black Nymo beading thread, size B
Two beading needles, size 12
Knitted scarf, approximately 7½" (19 cm) wide and 4½' (137 cm) long*

Note: I knitted my own using the stockinette stitch and 5 skeins of Trendsetter Binario novelty yarn, 25 g balls (approximately 82 yd), and size 9 needles.

First Fringe

a. Thread a needle onto each end of a 6 yd (549 cm) length of thread. Pass both needles through one end of the edge of the scarf. Then pass both the needles through the loop made by the thread, and pull tight (lark's head knot; Fig. 1).

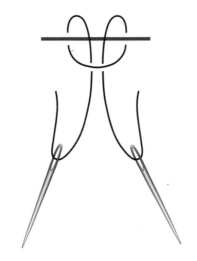

1. Lark's head knot with first thread.

b. Pass both threads through 1 amethyst chip, 1 blue iris charlotte bead, 1 faceted aqua or peridot fire-polished bead, 1 blue iris charlotte bead, and 1 amethyst chip. Push the beads down so they are touching the fabric.

c. Separate the threads. String onto each thread separately: 2 jade seed beads, 2 emerald seed beads, 2 light blue two-cuts, 2 lavender-lined seed beads, 2 purple transparent seed beads, 2 lavender-lined seed beads, 2 light blue two-cuts, 2 emerald seed beads, and 2 jade seed beads. Twist the two beaded strands around each other about four times.

d. Then pass both threads through the one amethyst chip and 1 purple seed bead. Go back through the amethyst chip with both threads (Fig. 2).

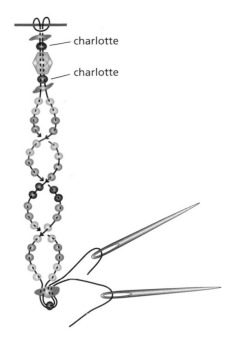

2. First half of the twisted fringe, starting to work back.

e. String onto each thread separately (Fig. 3): 2 jade seed beads, 2 emerald seed beads, 2 light blue two-cuts, 2 lavender-lined seed beads, 2 purple transparent seed beads, 2 lavender-lined seed beads, 2 light blue two-cuts, 2 emerald seed

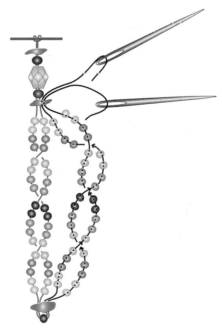

3. Making the second half of the twisted fringe. Working back towards the fabric.

beads, and 2 jade seed beads. Twist these two strands around each other about four times. Then pass both threads back up through the 2nd amethyst chip, 1 charlotte bead, 1 faceted fire-polished bead, 1 charlotte bead, and 1 amethyst chip at the top of the fringe, working toward the fabric (Fig. 3).

Second Fringe

Take a small stitch on the edge of the scarf with each needle, leaving enough room so that there is a space of about ¼" (6 mm) in between the fringes. Make the next fringe the same as the first one, but add a flower bead and a charlotte bead to the bottom (Fig. 4).

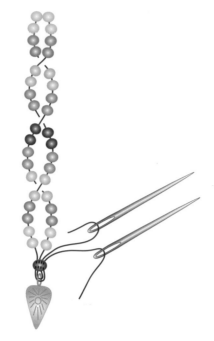

Third and Fourth Fringes

Make the third fringe exactly like the first one. Make the fourth fringe like the first one, but at the bottom, instead of an amethyst chip and a purple seed bead, add a blue iris charlotte bead and a silver charm (Fig. 5).

Repeat the four fringes all along the edge of the scarf until you come to the last group of fringes. Leave off the fourth fringe at the edge.

5. Silver charm ending of the first half of the fourth fringe.

4. Flower bead ending of the first half of the second fringe is added on.

Bead-Embroidered Scarf

MATERIALS

Teal green 9 mm bugle beads, 60
Green satin 4 mm bugle beads, 510
Delica beads as follows:
- Squash semi-matte, 5 g
- Silver-lined yellow, 5 g
- Lined pale pink, 5 g
- Silver-lined dark green, 5 g
- Opaque rose, 7 g
- Silver-lined dark ruby semi-matte, 7 g
- Silver-lined light green, 7 g

Black Nymo nylon monofilament beading thread, size F
Beading needle, size 11
Tracing paper
Erasable fabric marker
Tweezers
Black velvet scarf with fringe, at least 7½" (19 cm) wide

Flower and Leaves

1. Trace the design in Figure 1 onto tracing paper, using the fabric marker. Place the design on one end of the scarf, positioned well, and baste the paper in place. Embroider the beads onto the scarf through the paper, starting with the leaves, as follows:

a. The leaf outlines are made using the backstitch and the 4 mm bugle beads, with dark green Delica beads alternating with bugle beads. (See Chapter 2, section on how to backstitch with beads.)

b. The main vein of each leaf is backstitched using the teal green 9 mm bugle beads with a dark green Delica bead in between each pair of bugle beads.

Scarves have been worn around the neck for centuries. A scarf is said to be the precursor to the necktie. The orators of ancient Rome wore scarves around their necks to keep their voice boxes warm and functioning properly. Neck scarves didn't become high fashion until the middle of the 17th century, when the Croatian army marched into Paris wearing colorful scarves around their necks. King Louis XIV of France fell in love with the scarves, which were much more comfortable to wear than the fashionable collars of the time. The chrysanthemum design embroidered on this scarf was inspired by chrysanthemum themes used in Asian art.

c. For the secondary veins on the leaves, use the backstitch and the light green Delica beads only.

2. Using the satin stitch, embroider the lined pale pink, rose, and dark ruby arches of the petals. (See Chapter 2 for how to do satin stitch with beads.) Do the arches only at this point. The radiating lines are done later. Embroider the main yellow arch of the center of the flower using the satin stitch. Now embroider the other yellow arches, using the yellow beads and the backstitch.

3. Remove the tracing paper, using the tweezers for any hard-to-reach areas, and then backstitch the lines at the center of the flower with the squash Delica beads. Look at the photo for bead placement.

1. Chrysanthemum design chart, at 100%.

Figure 2. Fringe design chart.

4. Next, using the backstitch, embroider the radiating lines on the lined pink, rose, and ruby arches. There should be between 5 and 7 lines per arch. Check the photo for radiating line placement.

5. To make the fringe, thread the needle onto a 3 yd (274 cm) length of thread. Make a knot on the end of the thread, and pass the needle through the large knot on the first fringe group of the scarf's own fringe. Then:

a. String on the beads in this pattern (Fig. 2): 1 light green Delica bead, 1 green satin bugle bead, 1 light green Delica bead, *1 ruby, 1 rose, 1 pale pink, 1 yellow, 1 squash, 1 yellow, 1 pale pink, 1 rose, 1 ruby, 1 light green Delica bead, 1 green satin bugle bead, 1 light green, 1 green satin bugle bead, 1 light green Delica bead, 1 green satin bugle bead, 1 light green Delica bead.*

b. Repeat the pattern between the asterisks two times.

c. Add 1 ruby, 1 rose, 1 pale pink, 1 yellow, 1 squash, 1 yellow, 1 pale pink, 1 rose, 1 ruby, 1 light green Delica bead, 1 green satin bugle bead, and 1 light green Delica bead. Then skip the last bead strung on and pass the needle back through all the beads, going towards the fabric; tie a knot. Hide the excess thread in the beads, and trim off the thread end.

d. Repeat this pattern for all the other tassels. The pattern may have to be adjusted to fit your fringe length, by adding or removing design units.

Bead-Edged Silk Scarf

Ancient China was the first country to experience the soft, luxurious feel of silk. Five thousand years ago, as legend has it, Lady Hsi-Ling-Shih, wife of the Yellow Emperor, was having tea under a white mulberry tree. A cocoon from the silk moth, Bombyx mandarina, *fell from its perch in the tree and landed in her hot tea. The fiber began to unwind, and she discovered silk. Over the years, silk moths have been bred to produce the* Bombyx mori, *a blind, mouthless, flightless moth that only lives long enough to mate and lay eggs. The production of silk (sericul-ture) is a long and arduous task. First the eggs must be kept at the perfect temperature. When they hatch, the caterpillars must be fed freshly picked mulberry leaves every half-hour. After about a month they will have increased their weight by about 10,000 times. When the cocoons made by the caterpillars are ready, they are steamed to kill the caterpillar inside, and the silk is unwound. Each cocoon has a silk fiber that is over a half-mile long. These fibers are twisted together to make silk thread. The beaded V-edging on this lovely silk scarf adds just the right touch.*

MATERIALS

Multi-colored copper size 11° seed beads, 15 g

Black size 11° seed beads, 5 g

Light copper pearl size 6° seed beads, 124

Beading needle, size 11

Black Nymo nylon monofilament beading thread, size F

Light-colored erasable fabric marker

20″ × 20″ (51 × 51 cm) silk scarf

1. Mark all along the edge of the scarf every ½″ (1 cm) with the fabric marker.

2. Thread the needle on a 1 yd (1 m) length of thread. Tie a knot on the end, and pass the needle through the fabric at one of the corners, hiding the knot in the hem. String on 8 multi-colored size 11° copper beads, 1 black bead, 1 size 6° copper pearl bead, and then 1 black bead. Pass the needle back through the size 6° copper pearl bead and the first black bead strung on (Fig. 1). String on 8 multi-colored size 11° copper beads, and then make a little stitch at the ½″ (1 cm) mark (Fig. 2).

3. Keep edging this way. Repeat along all four sides of the scarf. At the end, make a double knot and hide the thread end in the seam allowance. Trim off thread ends.

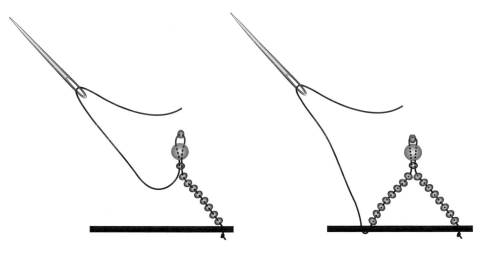

1. First half of the beaded V-edging.

2. Complete the V and make a little stitch at the ½″ (1 cm) mark.

Purple Flower Loomed Belt

Wampum belts have been woven by the Northeastern Native Americans for centuries. The beads that covered the belts were made from shells: white from the Atlantic whelk and purple and purplish-black from quahog clam shells. Wampum belts held significant political, social, and religious meaning. They were used for binding treaties and agreements and for historical record keeping. The Hiawatha Belt signifies the unity and the constitution of the Haudenosaunee (People Building a Long House), whom the French called the Iroquois. Legend has it that more than 500 years ago, Dekanawida, The Great Peacemaker, and his helper, Hiawatha, brought the five nations of the Haudenosaunee People together in peace and unity, with each nation keeping its own identity. The nations were the Onondaga (Fire Keepers and Wampum Keepers), the Mohawk or Kanienkehake (People of the Flint), the Seneca (People of the Great Hill), the Cayuga (People of the Swamp), and the Oneida (People of the Standing Stone). The wampum belts that the Haudenosaunee used in treaties with the Europeans were the "two-row" belts, which had two parallel rows of purple beads on a white background. The purple rows symbolized two boats traveling down the same river, the Native Americans and the Europeans, each with its own laws and culture. These unkept treaties were meant to ensure that the two boats would travel side by side, not interfering with each other. The design on this belt was inspired by the beautiful designs of Native American beadwork.

MATERIALS

Delica beads as follows:
- Light blue, 20 g
- Dark lavender, 15 g
- Silver-lined dark green, 10 g
- Dark purple, 7 g
- Dark mauve, 7 g
- Yellow, 5 g
- Lined hot pink, 5 g

Beading needle, size 11

Beading needle (short), size 11

Black Nymo nylon monofilament beading thread, size F

Bead loom

Thimble

Belt

1. See Chapter 2 for instructions on loom bead weaving. Warp the loom with 16 warp threads each 50″ (127 cm) long, using the black thread. Attach the weft thread to the left outermost warp thread, leaving a 2′ long (61 cm) tail for making the thread cloth later on. Then:

a. Use the size 11 beading needle to weave the beads, following the design chart in Figure 1 and reading it from left to right and from bottom to top.

b. Repeat the design 19 times or however many times it will take to fit your belt. The finished loomwork should measure ⅞″ (2 cm) wide and 25″ (64 cm) long, or whatever length you make it.

c. End by weaving ⅜″ (10 mm) of thread cloth to hold the beads tightly onto the warp threads. See Chapter 2, section on loom bead weaving, on how to make thread cloth.

d. Make a ⅜″ (10 mm) length of thread cloth on the starting side of the work. Remove the piece from the loom, and tie off all pairs of warp thread with square knots. Cut off the excess thread, and fold the thread cloth to the back of the work. If necessary, glue in place.

2. Sew the loomwork to the belt, using the short beading needle.

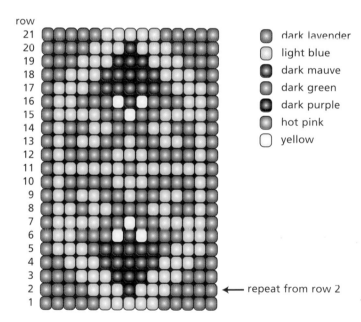

1. Design chart for Purple Flower Belt.
Repeat from second row to continue design.

Couched Leather Belt

Humans have been using animal skins as clothing for eons. In 1991, in the Otztal Alps on the border of Austria and Italy, a 5300-year-old man, one of the oldest and best preserved mummies ever found, was discovered by two hikers. He was wearing a leather jacket made of goat and deer hide, leather pants and shoes, and a bearskin hat, all extremely well preserved. Leather is still a popular material for making jackets, pants, shoes, purses, belts, wallets, and hats. Cowhide is the most common source, although many different animal skins can be used, including those of water buffalo, deer, elk, kangaroos, pigs, goats, sheep, horses, ostriches, snakes, lizards, eels, and seals. This couched and embroidered leather belt will add style to any wardrobe. The designs can be used on other fabrics and garments as well.

MATERIALS

White opal rondelles (round flat beads with center holes), 6

Irish emerald green size 11° two-cut beads, 7 g

Amethyst matte 12 mm bugle beads, 100

Light topaz matte AB (iridescent) 5 mm bugle beads, 60

Silver-lined lavender Delica beads, 5 g

Lined-crystal/yellow luster Delica beads, 5 g

Yellow-orange size 11° seed beads, 5

Green leaf beads, pendant style, 10

7" (18 cm) embroidery hoop

Beading needle, size 11

Beading needle (short), size 11

Straight pins

Thimble

Pliers

Tracing paper

Erasable fabric marker

Black Nymo nylon monofilament beading thread, size D

Suede belt

Flowers

1. Make 5 evenly spaced dots on the belt for the placement of centers of the flowers. Leave room on either side of each flower for the curly vines, and leave some space between each of the flower-and-vine units. Thread the short needle (shorts are stronger than the long beading needles and are easier to use with leather) with about 2 yd (183 cm) of thread. Make a knot on the end, and pass the needle through the suede up to the right side of the belt at one of the marked dots. You might want to use the pliers to help pull the needle through the leather. Then:

a. String on 1 rondelle and 1 yellow-orange seed bead. Pass the needle back through the white rondelle and the suede, making a stacked seed stitch. Bring the needle back up through the suede at a point next to the edge of the white rondelle.

b. To make an inner petal, string on 1 topaz bugle bead, 3 yellow luster Delica beads, and 1 topaz bugle bead (Fig. 1). Pass the needle back through the suede at a point right next to where the needle came out.

c. Make 5 more inner petals the same way around the white rondelle.

d. To make outer petals, make 10 looped fringes (petals) around the inner petals. Each petal is made by stringing on 1 amethyst bugle bead, 5 lavender Delica beads, and 1 amethyst bugle bead (Fig. 2). After you finish the flower, pass the needle back through the suede, tie a knot or two, and cut off the excess.

e. Create a flower 4 more times, one at each of the marked dots.

1. Inner petals, topaz looped fringe made of topaz bugle beads and yellow luster Delica beads.

2. Outer petals, purple looped fringe made of amethyst bugle beads and lavender Delica beads.

3. Vine design for tracing, at 100%. See photo for alignment.

Vines

2. The vines are attached by couching (see Chapter 2). To couch the vines, first trace the curved line for the left side of the design (Fig. 3) five times on 5 separate pieces of tracing paper. Then trace the line on the right side five times on 5 separate pieces of tracing paper. Then:

a. Pin the papers onto the belt at the sides of each flower. Place the section of the belt you want to work on into the embroidery hoop. Thread the needles (long and short) with about 3 yd (274 cm) of thread for each. Tie a knot on one end of each thread, and pass the long needle only up through the leather so that it is at a point at the beginning of one of the vine outlines. You will be stitching right through the paper.

b. String on about 3″ (8 cm) of emerald green two-cut beads. Push 3 or 4 beads down to the suede, depending on the shape of the line to be followed. Use more beads at a time to make a straight segment and fewer for curves.

c. Pass the short (couching) needle up through the suede at a point along the outline that will put it above the beaded thread, right next to the last bead pushed down. Pass the short needle back through the leather on the other side of the beaded thread, so its stitch catches the beaded thread.

d. Push more beads down on the beaded thread. Then pass the short needle back up through the suede and over the beaded thread and back down through the suede as you did in c.

e. Keep couching, adding more beads to the beaded thread as needed, until the vine outline is covered with beads. Repeat for all the vines, moving the embroidery hoop along the belt as necessary. Remove the tracing paper.

Leaves

Thread the short needle with about 1 yd (91 cm) of thread, and knot the end. Pass the needle up through the suede along one side of one of the vines (see photo for placement), and string on one leaf bead. Pass the needle back down through the suede, and tie a knot in back. Cut off the excess thread. Repeat 9 more times for two leaves per flower.

Hummingbird Knit Gloves

MATERIALS

Teal drop leaf beads, 4
Iris AB (iridescent) flower beads, 4
Teal silver-lined Delica beads, 4 g
Violet silver-lined Delica beads, 8 g
Cobalt (blue) silver-lined size 11° beads, 7 g
Silver hummingbird beads (pendants), 2
Black Nymo nylon monofilament beading thread, size D
Beading needle, size 11 or 12
Embroidery scissors
Pair of lavender knit gloves, or any color you want

See Chapter 2 for general instructions on vertical netting.

Base Strand

Make the base strand for the vertical net as follows:

■ Using about 3½ yd (320 cm) of thread, place a stop bead on one end. A stop bead is a bead temporarily tied onto the end of the thread to keep the other beads from falling off the thread. Then string on beads, repeating the pattern 1 violet bead and 1 cobalt bead, until there are 56 beads on the strand or enough beads to fit the width of the glove (Fig. 1).

Row 1

Get ready to start vertical row 1 of the net by skipping the last bead strung on and passing the needle back through the next 3 beads (Fig. 1). Then:

Gloves protect the hands from harsh environments and the hazards of sports. They keep the hands warm and are an integral element of fashion. Besides being practical and pretty, gloves have had many symbolic meanings over the centuries. The throwing down of a glove at someone's feet signified a challenge, and, for a time, wearing gloves represented wealth and power. Giving a glove was the same as giving your hand in love, challenge, or agreement. The gloves shown here are decorated using the vertical net stitch.

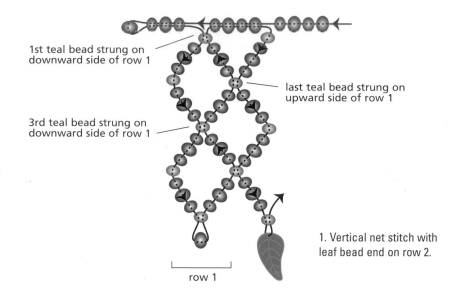

1st teal bead strung on
downward side of row 1

3rd teal bead strung on
downward side of row 1

last teal bead strung on
upward side of row 1

row 1

1. Vertical net stitch with
leaf bead end on row 2.

a. Downward side of row 1: *String on 1 teal, 1 violet, 1 cobalt, and 1 violet bead.* Repeat between the asterisks three times. Then string on 1 teal and 1 cobalt bead. Skip the cobalt bead, and then pass the needle back through the teal bead.

b. Upward side of row 1: **String on 1 violet, 1 cobalt, 1 violet, 1 teal, 1 violet, 1 cobalt, and 1 violet bead.** Then pass the needle back through the 3rd teal bead that you strung on the downward side of the row. Repeat between the double asterisks once, and then pass the needle back through first teal bead strung on the downward side of the row. This returns you to the base strand.

Row 2

Downward side of row 2: Pass the needle back through the next 4 beads on the base strand. Then string on 1 teal, 1 violet, 1 cobalt, and 1 violet bead. Then pass the needle through the last (nearest) teal bead that you strung on the upward side of row 1. String on 1 violet, 1 cobalt, 1 violet, 1 teal, 1 violet, 1 cobalt, and 1 violet bead. Pass the needle through the first teal bead strung on the upward side of row 1.

String on 1 violet, 1 cobalt, 1 violet, 1 teal, and 1 leaf bead. Pass the needle back through the teal bead (Fig. 1).

Upward side of row 2: String on 1 violet, 1 cobalt, 1 violet, 1 teal, 1 violet, 1 cobalt, and 1 violet bead. Then pass the needle back through the second teal bead strung on from the downward side of row 2. String on 1 violet, 1 cobalt, 1 violet, 1 teal, 1 violet, 1 cobalt, and 1 violet bead. Then pass the needle through the first teal bead strung on from the downward side of row 2. This returns you to the base strand. Pass the needle to the right through the next 4 beads on the base strand.

Row 3

Downward side of row 3: String on 1 teal, 1 violet, 1 cobalt, and 1 violet bead. Pass the needle back through the first teal bead strung on the upward side of row 2. String on 1 violet, 1 cobalt, 1 violet, 1 teal, 1 violet, 1 cobalt, and 1 violet bead. Then pass the needle through the first teal bead strung on the upward side of row 2. String on 1 violet, 1 cobalt, 1 violet, 1 teal, 1 violet, 1 cobalt, 1 violet, 1 teal, 1 violet,

1 cobalt, 1 violet, and 1 teal bead. Then string on 1 cobalt bead, and pass the needle through the teal bead.

Upward side of row 3: String on 1 violet, 1 cobalt, 1 violet, 1 teal, 1 violet, 1 cobalt, and 1 violet bead. Then pass the needle through the third teal bead strung on the downward side of row 3. String on 1 violet, 1 cobalt, 1 violet, 1 teal, 1 violet, 1 cobalt, and 1 violet bead. Then pass the needle through the second teal bead strung on the downward side of row 3. String on 1 violet, 1 cobalt, 1 violet, 1 teal, 1 violet, 1 cobalt, and 1 violet bead. Then pass the needle back through the first teal bead strung on the downward side of row 3.

Rest of the Rows

Keep working in the vertical net stitch with this same color pattern. Row 4 has 4 "stitches" or diamond-shaped holes, and the downward side of the row ends with a cobalt bead. Row 5 also has 4 stitches, but the downward side of the row ends with a flower bead and a cobalt bead (Fig. 2). Row 6 has 5 stitches, and the downward side ends with a cobalt bead. Row 7 has 6 stitches, and the downward side ends with a hummingbird bead and a cobalt

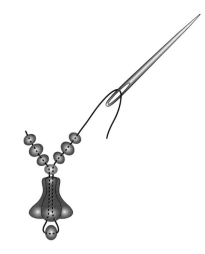

2. Flower bead end.

bead. Row 8 is the same as Row 6. Row 9 is the same as Row 5. Row 10 is the same as Row 4. Row 11 is the same as Row 3. Row 12 is the same as Row 2, and Row 13 is the same as Row 1.

End Triangles

To make the right end triangle, after you have made the last row, pass the needle to the right through the last 4 beads of the base strand. Then:

a. String on 1 teal, 1 violet, 1 cobalt, and 1 violet bead. Pass the needle through the last teal bead and the violet bead below it strung on the upward side of row 13, and pull tight. Make an overhand knot in between 2 beads (Fig. 3), and weave the thread upwards through the beads on several of the "stitches" until the thread is near the base strand. Then pass the needle through the base strand until the needle is coming out of the last bead on the other side (left) of the base strand.

b. To make the left end triangle, string on 1 teal, 1 violet, 1 cobalt, and 1 violet bead. Then pass the needle through the 2nd teal bead strung on the downward side of row 1.

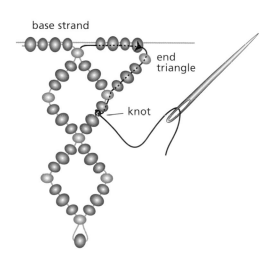

3. Overhand knot and finishing the right end triangle.

c. Make an overhand knot in between two beads (Fig. 3), and weave the thread through several of the "stitches" until the thread is coming out of the end bead of the base strand. Use this thread end to sew the beads onto the glove. Hide the other thread end by weaving it into several stitches. Somewhere along the line, make an overhand knot in between 2 beads. Cut off any excess thread.

Attaching the Netting

Place the netting on the glove with the base strand running along the edge of the cuff. Then:

a. Use the thread that is coming out of the base strand, and sew the netting onto the glove using the running stitch. Pass the needle through the fabric, make a small stitch to catch the fabric, pull the needle back out of the fabric, and pass the needle through the 3rd and 4th bead on the base strand. Pull tight.

b. Repeat across the glove, making stitches that are about a 2-bead length until you reach the end of the base strand.

c. Pass the needle through to the back side of the fabric. Make a knot, and then bring the needle back to the right side of the glove. Hide the end of the thread through the beads until it is secure. Cut off the excess.

Make the second glove in the same way you made the first glove.

Wild Winter Rose Gloves

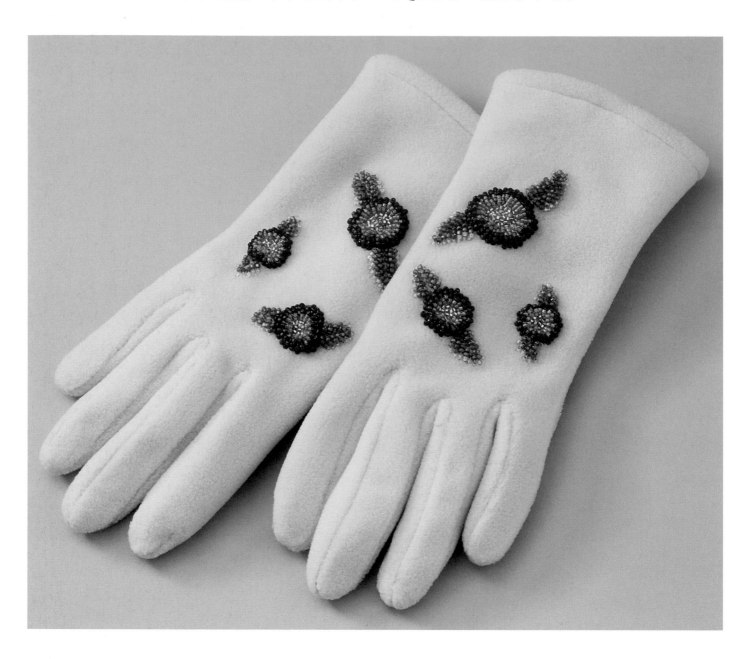

Rosa rugosa rubra *is deep pink in color and single-petaled, a hardy shrub that loves the sun but can handle some shade. This wild rose has sharp thorns and dark green leaves. It produces orange hips that birds find quite tasty. I wanted to* honor *this gorgeous rose by making it the center of attention on these warm and fuzzy gloves. This project is done in satin stitch, which gives the flowers and leaves a three-dimensional look. Decorate a scarf or hat with matching designs if you wish.*

MATERIALS

Silver-lined rose matte size 11° seed
    beads, 10 g
Silver-lined teal matte size 11° seed
    beads, 5 g
Pink-lined Delica beads, 10 g
Lined gold Delica beads, 125
Silver-lined aqua size 11° Japanese
    seed beads, 125
Beading needle, size 11
White Nymo nylon monofilament
    beading thread, size D
Pair of white fleece gloves, or any
    color you like
Tracing paper
Erasable fabric marker

1. Trace the design (Fig. 1) onto tracing paper using the fabric marker. Cut out the roses and leaves.

1. Wild winter rose design chart for left glove at 100%.
Flop design for right glove.

Pin the pieces onto the top side of the left glove in the arrangement seen in the photo. Trace around the pieces with the fabric marker. The roses will look like doughnuts, and the leaves will have a triangular shape. Then remove the pieces of tracing paper. See the general instructions for satin stitch.

Medium Flower

2. Start with the medium-sized flower, which is farthest away from the glove opening. Knot the end of a 2 yd (183 cm) length of thread. Keeping the glove right-side out, bring the needle into the glove and up and out at a point on the inside circle of the doughnut shape. We'll be making lines from the yellow circle outward with beads in satin

stitch (see general satin stitch instructions in Chapter 2):

a. String on 2 pink and 3 rose seed beads. Pass the needle through the point on the outside circle of the doughnut directly opposite the place where the needle first came out. Pull tight, pushing the needle inside the glove, and then pass the needle through the fabric at a point on the inside circle right next to the first line of beads.

b. String on 2 pink and 3 rose seed beads. Pass the needle back through the fabric at a point on the outside circle next to the first beads sewn on. The beads will be arched up (they won't be totally flat); that is how they are supposed to look.

c. Keep using the satin stitch and 2 pink and 3 rose seed beads, working your way around the circle until the whole outer circle of the flower is filled in.

3. Fill in the center of the medium flower randomly with about 14 gold Delica beads, using the seed stitch. When you are finished, knot the thread on the inside of the glove, hide the end of the thread in the fabric, and cut off the excess thread.

Closeup of medium flower.

Leaves

4. For the leaves of the medium flower (Fig. 2), use 2 yd (183 cm) of thread. Mark a center line on each leaf from the tip to the base. Knot the thread end, and pass the needle up through the fabric from the inside of the glove, so it comes out of the fabric at a point on the middle of the base of the leaf nearest the flower. We'll work from the center line outward in horizontal satin stitch lines.

2. Leaf design chart (half pattern) for the medium flower leaf. Work in lines from the center line out in satin stitch.

a. String on 3 teal beads and 1 aqua seed bead. Pass the needle back down through the fabric at a point on the outside edge of the leaf shape, where the end of the beads falls on the traced line. Then bring the needle back up out of the fabric at a point on the middle line of the leaf right above the first line of beads.

b. Using the satin stitch, keep progressing by adding lines of beads going up one side of the leaf towards the point:

- Use 2 teal and 1 aqua seed bead for the next 2 lines.
- Use 1 teal and 1 aqua seed bead for the next 2 lines.
- Then sew 1 aqua seed bead at the top point of the leaf.

c. Using the satin stitch, add horizontal lines of beads down the other side of the leaf, mirroring the first side.

d. When you are finished, tie a knot inside the glove, and hide the excess thread in the fabric.

e. Repeat Step 4 on the other side of the flower to make the second leaf.

Small Flower

5. Make the small flower the same way you made the medium-sized flower, except string on 2 pink and 2 rose seed beads for the lines of the petals, and fill in the center using

about 11 gold Delica beads. Make the leaves the same way you made the medium-sized leaves, but use 2 teal and 1 aqua seed bead for the first 2 lines of beads, and use 1 teal and 1 aqua seed bead for the last 2 lines of beads.

Large Flower

6. Make the large flower the same way you made the other two, except string on 3 pink and 3 rose seed beads for the lines of the petals, and fill in the center using about 37 gold Delica beads. The leaves of the large flower are made in the same way as the other leaves, except for the following: use 3 teal and 2 aqua seed beads for the first 3 lines, 3 teal and 1 aqua seed bead for the next 2 lines, 2 teal and 1 aqua seed bead for the next line, and 1 teal and 1 aqua seed bead for the last 2 lines.

7. Repeat Steps 1 to 6 for the other glove, being sure to flop the designs so they are a mirror image before tracing them.

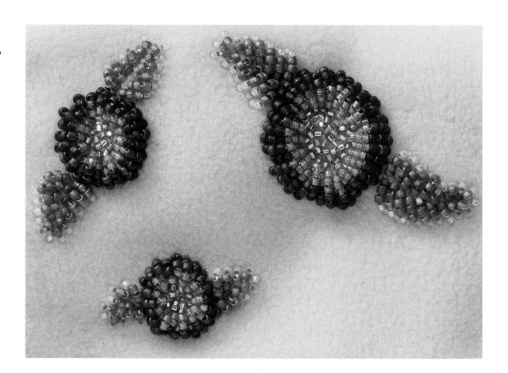

Tatted Bobby Socks

Bobby socks were introduced in the United States during World War II. Most of the nylon produced during the war went to make parachutes, so hose were scarce. Girls started wearing bobby socks (short, ankle-length socks), and by the 1950s they were all the rage. Bobby socks got their name from the word bob, which means to cut short or reshape. The word sock comes from the Middle English word socke, which comes from the Old English word socc, which means a light shoe, which comes from the Latin word soccus, which might possibly come from the Greek words sunkhis and sukkhos. Whatever the etymology, this cute tatted flower will surely knock your bobby socks off. It also would go well on a summer hat, a cloth tote, or a sweater.

MATERIALS

Seed beads as follows:
- Soft pink size 10°, 90
- Red AB (aurora borealis) size 11°, 40
- Yellow size 11°, 10

Silver-lined dark green Delica beads, 54

Silver-lined light green Delica beads, 54

Ball of dusty rose cotton crochet thread, size 10

Ball of green cotton crochet thread, size 10

Twisted wire bead needle

Tatting needle, size 5

White Nymo nylon monofilament beading thread, size D

Pair of white cotton ankle socks

Embroidery scissors

Flower

1. The flower is made of 5 rings and 5 chains, joined into a circle. Thread the rose crochet thread onto the twisted beading needle. String the beads onto the ball in this order: 23 pink, 1 red, 1 yellow, 1 red, 23 pink, 3 red, 1 yellow, 1 red, 23 pink, 3 red, 1 yellow, 1 red, 23 pink, 3 red, 1 yellow, 1 red, 23 pink, 3 red, 1 yellow, and 3 red beads. (You are stringing on the beads in the reverse order to the way they will be used.) Remove the twisted beading needle, and thread on the tatting needle. Start tatting about 20″ (51 cm) from the needle. See the section in Chapter 2 on how to tat with beads for general instructions.

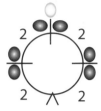

1. First bead-tatted ring.

2. To make the first ring (Fig. 1), follow this pattern: 2 double stitches, 2-bead picot, 2 double stitches, 3-bead picot, 2 double stitches, 2-bead picot, 2 double stitches; then close the ring (cl), and reverse the work (rw).

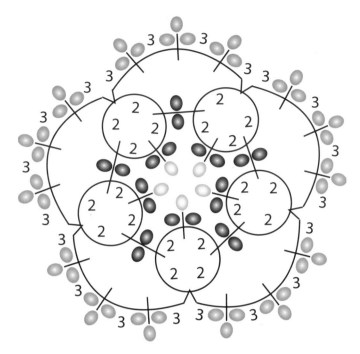

3. Five beaded rings and 5 beaded chains make up the tatted flower.

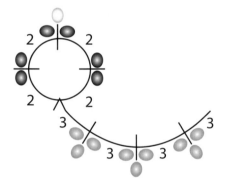

2. Bead-tatted ring and chain.

3. To make the chain (Fig. 2) that is connected to the ring you just made, follow this pattern: *3 double stitches, 3-bead picot, 3 double stitches, 3-bead picot, 3 double stitches, 3-bead picot, 3 double stitches; then close the ring and reverse the work. To make the second ring, follow this pattern: 2 double stitches, join (J) to the second 2-bead picot on the previous ring, 2 double stitches, 3-bead picot, 2 double stitches, 2-bead picot, 2 double stitches; then close the ring and reverse the work.* Repeat between the asterisks two times.

4. From the 4th ring, make another chain using the same pattern as before. For the last ring, follow this pattern: 2 double stitches, join to the second 2-bead picot from the previous ring, 2 double stitches, 3-bead picot, 2 double stitches, and then join to the first 2-bead picot from the first ring to form a circle. Then close the ring and reverse the work.

5. Make another chain from the 5th ring, using the same pattern as before. To connect the chain to the first ring and to form the flower, pass the needle through the very first 2 double stitches from the first ring, and tie a knot. Hide the excess thread through several stitches, and then cut off the excess. You should have 5 rings and 5 chains (Fig. 3).

Leaves

6. Make the leaves using the green crochet thread (Fig. 4). Make 2 leaves for each sock, a large one with light green beads and a small one with dark green beads as follows:

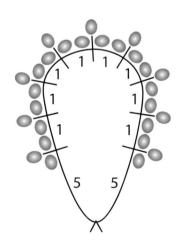

4. Large bead-tatted leaf uses light green beads.

a. Thread the twisted beading needle onto the ball of crochet thread, and string on 27 light green beads. Remove the twisted beading needle, and thread on the tatting needle.

b. Start tatting about 15″ (38 cm) from the needle. The light green, large leaf follows this pattern: 5 double stitches, *3-bead picot, 1 double stitch.* Repeat between the asterisks eight times, and then make 5 double stitches for a total of nine 3-bead picots. Close the ring, and tie a square knot. Hide the excess thread through several stitches, and cut off the remainder.

c. To make the small leaf, thread the twisted beading needle back onto the ball, and string on 27 dark green beads. Change to the tatting needle, and start tatting about 15″ (38 cm)

away from the needle. The small leaf (Fig. 5) follows this pattern: 3 double stitches, *3-bead picot, 1 double stitch.* Repeat between the asterisks seven times, and then make 3 double stitches for a total of eight 3-bead picots. Close the ring, and tie a square knot. Hide the excess thread through several stitches, and cut off the excess.

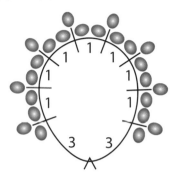

5. Small bead-tatted leaf uses dark green beads.

Attaching the Designs

7. Use the white beading thread and the embroidery needle to sew the flower and leaves onto the cuff on the outside of the sock. This ensures that the flowers will be visible on both socks when worn. See the photo for placement of leaves and flowers.

8. Repeat all the above steps to decorate the other sock.

Closeup of tatted flower and leaves.

Sheep Socks

Oh, for the love of sheep! Sheep are soft and cuddly-looking. Their wool is very thick and oily to the touch. The oil, which comes from the sheep's skin, provides protection from the environment. After the sheep is shorn, the wool is scoured in a tub of hot water and detergent to extract the dirt and the oil. The extracted oil is made into lanolin. The dried wool is carded to straighten the fibers and get it ready for the next step, spinning into yarn. Coarse wool is spun into woolen yarn, and fine wool is spun into worsted yarn. Breeds such as Merino have the finest wool; the Cheviot breed of sheep has coarse wool. Fine wool is used to make apparel, and the coarser wool is used in carpets and upholstery. Wool is the only fiber that is naturally flame-retardant. The sheep on these socks have wool made with the looped backstitch.

MATERIALS

Size 14° seed beads as follows:
- White opal luster, 5 g
- Black, 5 g
- Blue, 2
Beading needle, size 12
Black Nymo nylon monofilament beading thread, size D
White Nymo nylon monofilament beading thread, size D
Embroidery scissors
Pair of beige socks without cuffs, or other color
Tracing paper
Erasable fabric marker

1. Trace the sheep diagram (Fig. 1). Cut it out for a template, and place it on the upper part of one sock, making sure the sheep faces toward the toe of the sock. When doing the other sock, make sure to place the sheep on the opposite side of the sock, and flop the pattern. This way the sheep will be visible when the socks are worn. Use the marking pen to trace around the sheep template on the sock. Remove the template, and mark the face and ear area.

1. Sheep design diagram at 100%.

White Wool Area

2. Use about 3 yd (274 cm) of white beading thread to bead the wool area:

a. To knot the thread end, first make a small stitch on the inside of the sock, and then make a square knot and a half (Fig. 2).

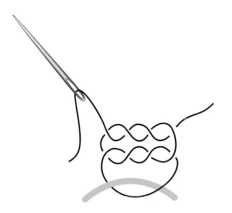

2. Square knot and a half.

b. For filling in the white wool area, use the looped backstitch (Fig. 3). The size of the stitch is smaller than the length of the beads would be if they were placed next to each other, causing the beads to form a loop. Each stitch or loop consists of 3 white seed beads (Fig. 3; see Chapter 2 for more details about the looped backstitch).

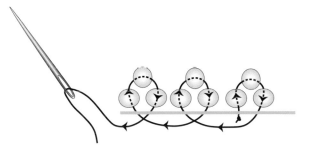

3. Looped backstitch.

c. First outline the wool area with the looped backstitch, and then go around and around inside of the outline until the entire wool area is full of beads. Leave a small space between stitches so the fabric will lie flat; if the stitches are too close together, the fabric will bunch up. Be sure to begin and end the thread with a square knot and a half so the knots can't escape.

Face, Legs, and Ear

3. Change to black thread and the backstitch to do the face and legs.

a. Outline a leg with backstitch (Fig. 4; also see Chapter 2 section on backstitch). Then fill in the middle section in backstitch. Repeat for each leg.

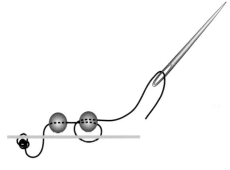

4. Backstitch.

b. Outline the face area with backstitch, and then fill in the area with two lines of backstitch. Use a blue bead instead of a black one for the eye (Fig. 5).

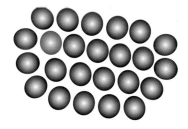

5. Eye placement chart.

4. To make the ear, bring the needle out of the fabric at the top point of the ear mark on Fig. 1, string on 7 black beads, and pass the needle back through the fabric at the bottom point of the ear mark. This creates a loop for an ear. Knot off, and cut off excess thread.

Note: The sheep will expand as it is made and will be bigger than the template; this is normal. As sheep are in real life, each sheep you make will be unique.

5. Make the second sock in the same way you made the first one.

Daisy Chain Canvas Shoes

Rubber-soled canvas shoes are a fairly recent fashion phenomenon. In the mid-1800s, Charles Goodyear invented vulcanized rubber, originally to make waterproof mailbags. Soon it was found that vulcanized rubber was perfect for shoe soles. Only the rich could afford such shoes at first, and they were worn for croquet and tennis. By the late 1800s, prices had become reasonable, and they were selling well. People began to call these shoes sneakers, because no one could hear you coming when you wore them. They have also been called felonies, creepers, gumshoes, gym shoes, trainers, tennis shoes, daps, athletic shoes, and plimsolls. Today, many people call them by their brand names. By whatever name, the rubber-soled canvas shoe is definitely entrenched in today's fashion world. This daisy chain edging will add personality to any shoe.

MATERIALS

Turquoise AB size 11° seed
  beads, 7 g
Copper size 11° seed beads, 5 g
Light copper matte size 8° seed
  beads, about 36*
Disappearing ink fabric marker
Beading needle, size 11
White Nymo nylon monofilament
  beading thread, size D (or
  whatever color matches your
  shoes)
Pair of tennis shoes (sneakers)

*Note: The number of beads varies,
depending on the size of the shoes.*

1. Mark along the edge of the shoe opening every ½″ (1 cm) with the fabric marker. Try to make the marks as close to the stitching holes that attach the edge to the shoe as you can, or on those holes. This makes it much easier to push the needle through the canvas because the needle goes through the hole already made. See closeup photo.

a. Thread the needle onto a 3′ (1 m) length of thread. Tie a knot on the end, and pass the needle through the seam allowance on the inside of the shoe near the first ½″ (1 cm) mark, to hide the knot. Then pass the needle through the canvas to the outside of the shoe at the first ½″ (1 cm) mark.

b. *String on 5 turquoise and 10 copper size 11° beads. Pass the needle back through the first copper bead strung on, forming a circle (Fig. 1). String on a size 8° bead, and then pass the needle back through the 6th size 11° copper bead strung on. String on 5 turquoise beads. Pass the needle through a stitch hole near the next ½″ (1 cm) mark you made, and bring the needle to the inside of the shoe.*

c. Pass the needle through the next stitch hole, and bring the needle to the outside of the shoe.

d. Repeat between the asterisks (b) as many times as are needed to decorate around the opening of your shoe.

e. To fill in the gaps at the top between the daisy chain fringes, use the running stitch hidden in the seam allowance and place one size 11° copper bead in each gap.

2. Repeat the instructions to decorate the other shoe.

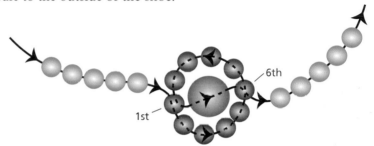

1. Daisy chain stitch.

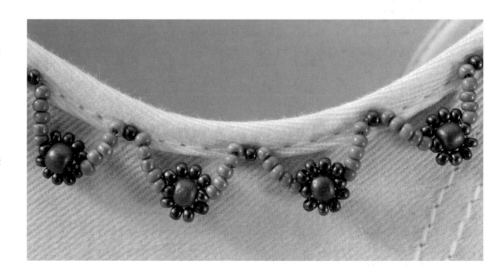

Daisy Chain Sandals

Traditional Japanese footwear includes zori. The zori is a sandal with a flat sole made from woven tatami and rubber. Tatami is a woven mat or cloth that has a reed cover, straw middle, and cloth edging. Zoris are held onto the foot with a V-shaped strap between the toes. The zoris in this project are decorated with a daisy chain. This daisy chain would be pretty on a belt also.

MATERIALS*

Pink swirl 5 mm druk beads (very round glass beads), 26

Silver-lined amber size 5° seed beads, 112

Light green AB (iridescent) size 5° seed beads, 96

Dark green 7 mm diamond-shaped Chinese glass crystal beads, 32

Black Nymo nylon monofilament beading thread, size F

Beading needle, size 11

Bonding glue

Pair of zori sandals

The number of beads you will need varies, depending on the size of the sandals.

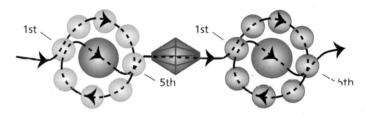

1. Daisy-chain stitch for sandals, showing amber and light green daisies.

The daisy chain is beaded first and then glued and stitched to the sandal.

1. Use about 3 yd (274 cm) of thread. String on 8 amber beads (Fig. 1). Leave a tail of about 8″ (20 cm). Pass the needle back through the first bead strung on to form a circle. Keep the tension tight, and string on 1 pink druk bead. Pass the needle through the 5th bead strung on, and pull tight. This makes an amber daisy.

2. String on 1 dark green crystal bead.

3. String on 8 light green seed beads. Pass the needle back through the first light green bead (Fig. 1). String on 1 pink druk bead. Pass the needle back through the 5th light green bead strung on. This makes a light green daisy.

4. String on 1 dark green crystal bead.

5. Continue alternating amber and light green daisies, adding a green crystal bead between them. Measure the distance from the center front of the shoe to the farthest edge of the side piece, where it joins the sole. When you create enough daisy chain so that you only lack one pattern to make that distance, string on 3 dark green crystal beads. Then do the center daisy and string on another 3 dark green crystal beads.

6. Continue to create beaded daisy chain as you did for the first side of the shoe, alternating daisy colors until you have a long enough chain for the second side too.

7. Tie off, and then weave the thread end through several daisies to hide and secure it. Do the same to the 8″ (20 cm) tail of thread left at the beginning.

8. Glue the central amber daisy to the center of the sandal strap to hold it in place, and then sew the rest of the daisy chain onto the straps.

9. Repeat Steps 1 through 8 to decorate the other sandal.

Dragonfly Slippers

Dragonflies belong to the order Odonata, which comes from the Greek word for tooth, odon. Dragonflies have "teeth" and are aggressive predators. Dragonflies are usually larger than damselflies and are much better fliers. They have four wings that can move independently, allowing them to fly backward, forward, up, down, and sideways. They can also hover and fly very fast, which makes them hard to catch.

Dragonflies have been a source of superstition around the world for centuries. Most of these superstitions are reflected in the different common names for dragonflies. The dragonfly has been called the darner, devil's darning needle, sewing needle, ear sewer, darning needle, spindle, blind stinger, devil's horse, and devil's needle. These names came from old superstitions that dragonflies are sent to the earth by the devil to cause harm and that they can sew up your ears, puncture your eardrum, poke out your eyes, or sew your eyelids shut.

But dragonflies are very beautiful, as anyone who has ever seen their delicate wings gleaming in the sunlight can tell. Dragonfly motifs have been used to decorate jewelry, ceramics, textiles, and many other things for centuries. Slippers with these bead-embroidered dragonflies make a great gift. This is a good project for getting rid of leftover beads.

1. Trace the design onto the tracing paper (Fig. 1). Baste the tracing paper onto the left slipper, centering the design on the slipper front (see photo). With about 2 yd (183 cm) of thread, backstitch on the stems using an assortment of bugle beads and the green silver-lined ⅛" bugle beads, following the design. See Chapter 2 for general notes on how to do bead backstitch.

1. Dragonfly design pattern at 100%.

MATERIALS *

Blue dagger beads for the wings, 8
Turquoise transparent disk beads for the thoraxes, 2
Black faceted 3 mm beads for the eyes, 4
Black iris faceted 5 mm beads for the heads, 2
Purple AB hex beads, 6
Black 5 mm bugle beads, 4
Size 11° seed beads as follows:
  • Gold-lined, 4
  • Light lavender, 4
  • Yellow, for dark pink and purple flower centers, 8
  • Pearly pink, for fuchsia flower centers, 4
  • Red, for yellow flower centers, 18
  • White, for yellow flower centers, 6
Purple metallic size 8° seed beads, 4

Light green leaf beads, 10
Flower beads as follows:
  • Dark pink 10 mm, 4
  • Fuchsia 7 mm, 4
  • Purple 8 mm, 2
  • Cobalt blue 6 mm pendant, 2
  • Yellow transparent 17 mm, 2
Green silver-lined ⅛" bugle beads for grass and stems, 7 g
Assorted green bugle beads for stems, 32
Beading needle, size 11
Pair of off-white slippers, or other light color
White Nymo nylon monofilament beading thread, size D, or thread to match slippers
Tracing paper
Erasable fabric marker
Tweezers

Note: You can substitute beads you have handy or some of your favorites.

Flowers

2. Make the flowers as follows:

a. Stitch the flower by passing the needle through the slipper from inside out at the point on the design where a flower center is, and then stitch through the center of a flower bead (Fig. 2). String on 1 size 11° seed bead, and then pass the needle back through the center of the flower. Repeat to make other flowers (see photo for reference). The cobalt blue flower bead doesn't have a center hole, so just sew it on.

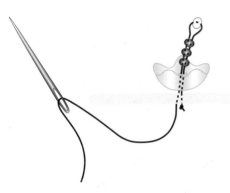

2. Making a yellow flower stamen.

b. To make a center stamen of the yellow flower, pass the needle through the slipper at the point on the design where the yellow flower is, and then pass the needle through the center of the flower. *String on 3 red seed beads and 1 white seed bead. Pass the needle back through the 3 red beads, through the center of the flower, and through the slipper (Fig. 2). Make a small stitch, and then pass the needle back through the slipper and back through the center of the same flower.* Repeat between the asterisks 2 times to make 2 more stamens for that flower.

Dragonfly and Other Parts

3. Make the dragonfly by seed-stitching the head, eyes, wings, and thorax as follows:

a. For the head, use the black iris faceted size 5 mm bead. For the eyes, use the black faceted size 3 mm beads. For the thorax, use the

turquoise disk bead. For the wings, use the blue dagger beads.

b. For the long abdomen, use the backstitch and the beads in this order, working from just behind the head downwards: 1 purple hex bead, 1 black bugle bead, 1 light lavender seed bead, 1 gold seed bead, 1 purple size 8° seed bead, 1 purple hex bead, 1 purple size 8° bead, 1 gold seed bead, 1 light lavender seed bead, 1 black bugle bead, and 1 purple hex bead.

4. Sew on 5 leaf beads as shown in the diagram. Use the assorted-length bugle beads to make grass.

5. Remove the tracing paper, using the tweezers.

6. Make the line of grass along the edge of the slipper, using the small green bugle beads and the backstitch (see photo).

7. Repeat Steps 1 through 6 for the other slipper, but make sure you flop the design before tracing so it will be a mirror image of the first slipper.

Tatted Purse

In the 1800s, long, narrow miser's bags with a very slender middle were a popular type of purse. They were usually knitted or crocheted and were used to hold coins. There was a slit opening in the slender middle with one or two metal rings that slid down to hold the coins in place. There were no handles, and the bags were made to be either slung over a belt or waistband or held in the hand. The name miser's bag arose because only two fingers would fit in to retrieve the money, once the ring was slid out of the way of the opening. Whatever style of bag you choose to decorate, the tatted medallions shown here can be made quickly and are fun to make.

MATERIALS*

Burgundy iridescent size 11° seed beads, 5 g

Burgundy cotton crochet thread, size 10

Tatting needle, size 5

Twisted beading needle, size medium

Embroidery scissors

Embroidery needle

Crocheted or cloth purse

Sewing thread to match your purse

Eyeglass or cell phone case (optional)

Note: Adapt the color of the thread and beads to suit your purse color.

Large Medallion

1. See Chapter 2 for general instructions on how to tat with beads. To make the large medallion for the purse, string 115 burgundy seed beads onto the crochet thread ball, using the twisted beading needle. Remove the twisted beading needle, and thread on the size 5 tatting needle. Start tatting about 20″ (51 cm) from the needle, as follows:

a. To make the first ring (Fig. 1), follow this pattern: 2 double stitches, 6-bead picot, 3 double stitches, 6-bead picot, 2 double stitches; then close the ring (cl), and reverse the work (rw).

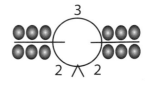

1. The first bead-tatted ring.

b. To make the chain (Fig. 2), follow this pattern: *3 double stitches, 3-bead picot, 3 double stitches, 5-bead picot, 3 double stitches, 7-bead picot, 3 double stitches, 5-bead picot, 3 double stitches, 3-bead picot, 3 double stitches; then close ring and reverse the work.

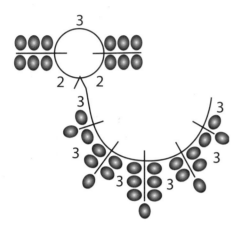

2. Adding the bead-tatted chain.

c. The second ring (Fig. 3) follows this pattern: 2 double stitches, join to the second 6-bead picot on the previous ring you made, 3 double stitches, 6-bead picot, 2 double stitches; then close the ring and reverse the work.*

d. Repeat between the asterisks (b and c) two times.

e. Make a chain as in b. Then for the last ring, follow this pattern: 2 double stitches, join to the 2nd 6-bead picot from the previous ring, 3 double stitches, then join to the first 6-bead picot from the first ring to form a circle. Then close the ring and reverse the work. Make another chain as in b.

f. To connect the last chain to the first ring and to form the medallion, pass the needle through the very first 2 double stitches from the first ring and tie a knot. Hide the excess thread through several stitches, and then cut off the excess (Fig. 3).

Large Tri-Rings

2. Next, make the large tri-rings that are placed around the large medallion. Using the twisted beading needle, string 87 burgundy seed beads onto the crochet thread ball. Remove the twisted beading needle, and thread on the size 5 tatting needle. Start tatting about 15″ (38 cm) from the needle as follows:

a. For the first ring, follow this pattern: 5 double stitches, 3-bead picot, 2 double stitches, 3-bead picot, 2 double stitches, 5-bead picot, 2 double stitches, 7-bead picot, 2 double stitches, 5-bead picot, 2 double stitches, 3-bead picot, 2 double stitches, 3-bead picot, 5 double stitches; then close ring.

b. Make two more rings, following the same pattern as the first ring. Hide the thread end through several stitches, and then cut off the excess. Make four more of these large tri-rings for a total of five for the purse front.

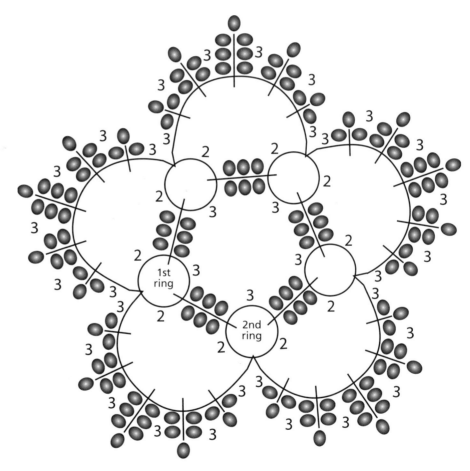

3. The large medallion.

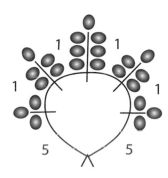

4. The first bead-tatted ring on the small tri-rings under the strap.

Small Tri-Rings

3. To make a small tri-ring that is to be placed right below a handle on the purse front, string 69 burgundy seed beads onto the crochet thread ball, using the twisted beading needle. Remove the twisted beading needle, and thread on the size 5 tatting needle. Start tatting about 15″ (38 cm) from the needle as follows (Fig. 4):

a. For the first ring, follow this pattern: 3 double stitches, 3-bead picot, 1 double stitch, 5-bead picot, 1 double stitch, 7-bead picot, 1 double stitch, 5-bead picot, 1 double stitch, 3-bead picot, 3 double stitches; then close ring.

b. Make two more rings following the same pattern (a) as the first ring. When done, hide the thread end through several stitches, and then cut off the excess.

c. Make one more small tri-ring to go below the other handle.

Attaching Tatting

4. Sew the large medallion onto the center front of the purse. Then sew on the five large tri-rings, evenly spaced around the large medallion, making sure that a point of each tri-ring triangle points outward from the medallion. Next sew each of the two small tri-rings on the front near the bottom of a handle. The placement of the medallion and tri-rings may have to be adjusted to fit the purse if it is a different shape than the one shown.

5. If you wish, make and attach one more small tri-ring and one more large medallion for an eyeglass case or cell phone case.

Center medallion and large tri-rings.

Orchid Purse

A reticule is a small fabric purse that was popular in the late 19th century. Before that, women carried their things in pockets sewn into their dresses or attached to their waistbands, but as styles changed and full skirts became more stream-lined, it got harder to hide a pocket. Women began carrying their things in reticules. They were sometimes decorated with beads, embroidery, and other trimmings. Here is a purse decorated with loomed beadwork that would rival any reticule.

MATERIALS*

Delica beads, as follows:
- Olive green opaque AB (iridescent), 7 g
- Silver-lined yellow, 5 g
- Hot pink-lined, 7 g
- Dark mauve dyed opaque, 7 g
- White pearl, 10 g

Black Nymo nylon monofilament beading thread, size F

Maroon Nymo nylon monofilament beading thread, size F*

Beading needle (long), size 11

Beading needle (short), size 11

Beading loom

Scissors

Maroon purse, or whatever color you want

*Match thread to the color of the purse. Amounts of beads will vary, depending on the length of the purse strap.

1. See Chapter 2 for general instructions on how to do loom bead weaving. To make the beaded loomwork for the purse strap, warp the loom with 10 warp threads, each 5' (130 cm) long, using the black thread. Then:

a. Attach the weft thread to the left outermost warp thread, leaving a 2' (61 cm) long tail for making the thread cloth at the end later on.

b. Use the long size 11 beading needle to weave the beads, following the strap design chart (Fig. 1), reading it from left to right and bottom to top.

c. Repeat the design as many times as needed until the desired length is reached to fit your purse strap. The strap on our purse is ½" × 13½" (1 × 34 cm), and the design was repeated 5½ times.

d. End by weaving ⅜" (1 cm) of thread cloth to hold the beads tightly onto the warp threads. See loom bead weaving section in Chapter 2 for how to make thread cloth.

e. Make a ⅜" (1 cm) length of thread cloth on the other side of the work. Remove the piece from the loom, and tie off all pairs of warp threads with square knots. Cut off the excess thread, and fold the thread cloth to the back of the work. If necessary, tack in place.

2. Use the short size 11 beading needle (short needles are sturdier than the long beading needles) and beading thread the same color as the strap, in this case maroon. Sew the loomwork to the strap along the edges of the piece.

3. Make the ¾" × 2" (2 × 5 cm) beaded piece for the purse body, using 16 black warp threads, each 1 yd (1 m) long. Warp the loom. Then attach the weft thread to the left outermost warp thread, leaving a 24"

32 31 30 29 28 27 26 25 24 23 22 21 20 19 18 17 16 15 14 13 12 11 10 9 8 7 6 5 4 3 2 1

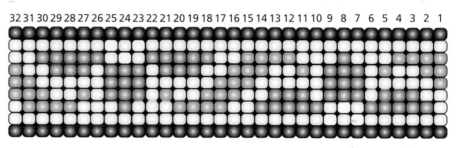

1. Strap design chart.

31 30 29 28 27 26 25 24 23 22 21 20 19 18 17 16 15 14 13 12 11 10 9 8 7 6 5 4 3 2 1

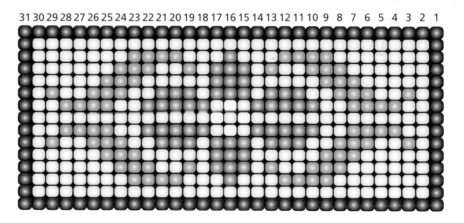

2. Orchid design chart for front of purse.

(61 cm) tail for making the thread cloth later on. Use the long size 11 beading needle to weave the beads, following the design chart (Fig. 2), reading it from left to right and bottom to top. Finish the loomed piece the same way as the one for the purse strap, and sew it to the center front of the purse, near the top.

- ● dark mauve
- ● olive green
- ● hot pink
- ○ yellow
- ○ white pearl

Bead-Fringed Umbrella

Umbrellas were originally used for protection from the harsh rays of the sun. The Thai word rom *means both* "umbrella" *and* "shade." *The Latin root word for umbrella is* umbra, *meaning shade. Parasol comes from the French words* parare, *meaning to shield, and* sol, *meaning sun. In ancient times in Egypt, China, India, Greece, and Rome, large umbrellas were used to protect rulers when they went out. The traditional paper*

umbrella of China, although as beautiful and fragile-looking as a butterfly's wing, is actually quite sturdy and can protect its owner from the harsh rays of the sun and the pelting rain. Our umbrella project uses a modern nylon umbrella, rimmed in fringed edging. Evenly spaced around the edge are large glass beads that resemble the clear purity of a raindrop.

MATERIALS

Lavender iris matte size 11° seed beads, 1 oz

Purple-lined iridescent size 11° seed beads, 1 oz

Lavender transparent 10 mm glass faceted beads, 24

Black Nymo nylon monofilament beading thread, size D

Beading needle, size 11

Umbrella

1. Umbrella fringe design chart.

1. Knot the end of a 3½ yd (320 cm) length of thread. Hide the knot in the hem of the umbrella next to one of the metal supports. Bring the needle out through the edge of the fabric close to the support (Fig. 1, left side). Then:

a. Small Fringe: *String on 2 lavender, 4 purple-lined, 1 lavender, and 1 purple seed bead. Pass the needle back through the third purple bead strung on. String on 2 purple and 2 lavender beads. Leave a space of about ¼″ (6 mm), and then make a small stitch, but not so small that the beads crowd each other.*

This makes the small fringe. Repeat between the asterisks two times.

b. Medium Fringe: **String on 3 lavender, 5 purple, 1 lavender, and 1 purple bead. Pass the needle back through the fourth purple bead strung on. String on 3 purple and 3 lavender beads. Leave a space of about ¼″ (6 mm), and make a small stitch.** This makes the medium-sized fringe. Repeat between the double asterisks once.

c. Large Fringe: String on 4 lavender, 6 purple, 1 lavender, and 1 purple bead. Pass the needle back through the fifth purple bead strung on.

Then string on 4 purple and 4 lavender beads. Leave a ¼″ (6 mm) space, and then make a small stitch. This makes the large fringe.

d. String on 4 lavender beads, 6 purple beads, one 10 mm glass bead, and one lavender bead. Pass the needle back through the 10 mm glass bead, and then string on one purple bead. Pass the needle back through the fifth purple bead strung on, and then string on 4 purple and 4 lavender beads. (Fig. 1 shows the completed pattern.)

e. ***Make 1 large, 2 medium, 3 small, 2 medium, 1 large fringe, and 1 large fringe with a glass bead on the end.*** Repeat between the triple asterisks once.

f. Make 1 large, 2 medium, and 3 small fringes. This is the end of the first section of the umbrella.

Note: The space in between the Vs might have to be adjusted in order for the fringe design to fit your umbrella section.

2. Repeat Step 1 for each of the other seven umbrella sections.

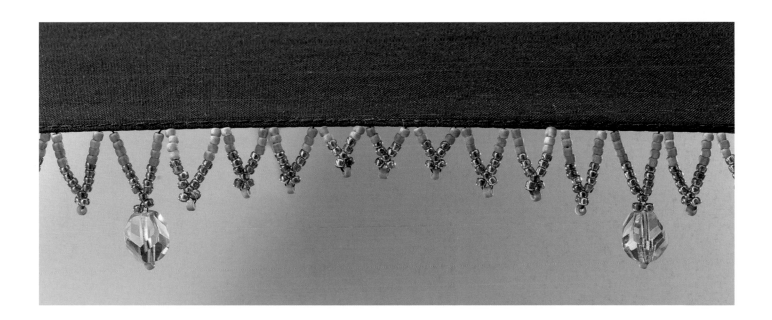

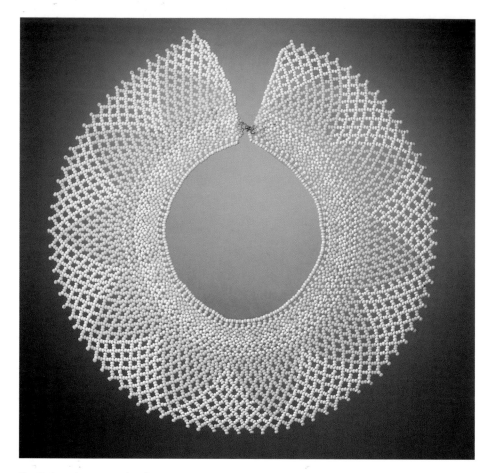

South American netted collar.

Kirdi beaded modesty apron, from Cameroon.

Romanian men's belt.

Middle Eastern hat.

Native American pouch with lane stitching.

Sioux strike-a-light bag.